Pocket
BANGKOK

TOP SIGHTS • LOCAL LIFE • MADE EASY

Austin Bush

In This Book

QuickStart Guide

Your keys to understanding the city – we help you decide what to do and how to do it

Need to Know
Tips for a smooth trip

Neighbourhoods
What's where

Explore Bangkok

The best things to see and do, neighbourhood by neighbourhood

Top Sights
Make the most of your visit

Local Life
The insider's city

The Best of Bangkok

The city's highlights in handy lists to help you plan

Best Walks
See the city on foot

Bangkok's Best...
The best experiences

Survival Guide

Tips and tricks for a seamless, hassle-free city experience

Getting Around
Travel like a local

Essential Information
Including where to stay

Our selection of the city's best places to eat, drink and experience:

◎ **Sights**

✖ **Eating**

🅟 **Drinking**

☆ **Entertainment**

🅐 **Shopping**

These symbols give you the vital information for each listing:

☎	Telephone Numbers	👪	Family-Friendly
⊙	Opening Hours	🐾	Pet-Friendly
🅟	Parking	🚌	Bus
🚭	Nonsmoking	⛴	Ferry
@	Internet Access	Ⓜ	Metro
📶	Wi-Fi Access	Ⓢ	Skytrain (BTS)
🌱	Vegetarian Selection	🚊	Tram
📖	English-Language Menu	🚆	Train

Find each listing quickly on maps for each neighbourhood:

Bar Hemingway

16 🅟 Map p233, B2

Legend has it that Hemi self, wielding a machine rate this timber-pan ered bar during showpiece is a en by Papa ar town. Dress s.com; Hôtel Rit ⊙6.30pm-2a

QuickStart Guide 7

Explore Bangkok 21

Worth a Trip:

The Best of Bangkok 139

Bangkok's Best Walks

Bangkok's Best ...

Survival Guide 161

TOM BONAVENTURE/GETTY IMAGES ©

QuickStart Guide

Welcome to Bangkok

Scratch Bangkok's surface and you'll find a city with mega-malls minutes from 200-year-old homes, with temples sharing space with neon-lit strips of sleaze, and where streets lined with food carts are overlooked by restaurants perched in skyscrapers. And best of all, as Bangkok races towards the future, these quirks will continue to supply the city with its unique brand of Thai-ness.

Monks at Wat Traimit (p60)
ELENA ERMAKOVA (LUNARLYNX)/GETTY IMAGES ©

Bangkok
Top Sights

Wat Phra Kaew & Grand Palace (p24)

Easily the most ostentatious temple in Thailand, Wat Phra Kaew blows minds with its blinged-out structures and Emerald Buddha. Next door, the Grand Palace is the equally decadent former residence of Thailand's royal family.

Wat Pho (p28)

At nearly 50m long and 15m high, it's impossible not to be awed by Wat Pho's reclining Buddha. And if you require more than just girth, the grounds are also home to a traditional massage school.

Jim Thompson's House (p74)

The eponymous American silk entrepreneur mysteriously disappeared in 1967, but his Thai-style former home lives on as a visit-worthy repository for ageing local traditions and artwork.

Chatuchak Weekend Market (p130)

In a city obsessed with commerce, Chatuchak takes the prize as Bangkok's biggest and baddest market. Silks, sneakers, fighting fish and fluffy puppies – if it can be sold in Thailand, you'll find it here.

Wat Arun (p32)

It's the setting by the river, rather than the gold or Buddha statues, that draws folks here. And justifiably – the views are great and Wat Arun is one of the few temples visitors can climb on.

Wat Traimit (Golden Buddha) (p60)

All the gold in Chinatown (and believe us, there's a lot) would scarcely be enough to re-create this nearly 6-tonne, solid-gold Buddha image. Let the jaw-dropping begin at this temple in Bangkok's Chinatown.

Ko Kret (p136)

Leave the city behind at this artificial yet thoroughly rural-feeling island in the Mae Nam Chao Phraya. Arrive on a weekend and combine your excursion with a busy open-air market and unique eats.

Dusit Palace Park (p56)

Witness Victorian sense and Thai sensibilities merging in this former royal enclave. Visit museums and the world's largest teak building, or simply take advantage of Dusit Palace Park's green setting – itself an anomaly in Bangkok.

Bangkok Local Life

Insider tips to help you find the real city

Don't want to feel like a sheltered package tourist? Rest assured that it's a cinch to get local in Bangkok, a city where hectic tourist attractions often rub shoulders with classic local neighbourhoods. Gay and lesbian travellers as well as foodies will also feel at home in Bangkok, a city as gay-tolerant as it is food-obsessed.

Banglamphu (p40)

▶ Fun bars
▶ Live music

Bangkok's most traditional 'hood is also one of its best for nightlife. Parts of Banglamphu can feel dominated by the backpacker magnet that is Th Khao San, but just off the main strip are heaps of bars, cafes and restaurants frequented by young locals.

Chinatown (p58)

▶ Street food
▶ Urban exploration

Many of the best places to eat have have neither roof nor menu, but it's not unusual for a Bangkokian to brave traffic, heat or rain for a meal in Chinatown. Not surprisingly, Chinese-style dishes rule here – think noodles, pork and fried dishes – but seafood, sweets and fruit also have their places.

Victory Monument (p90)

▶ Live music
▶ Regional Thai food

Want a taste of provincial Thailand without leaving Bangkok? Head to this suburban 'hood colloquially known for its main landmark. Here you'll find fun bars, live music and good food, from restaurants serving southern Thai to streetside stalls selling northeastern Thai specialities – all served up without a hint of big-city pretension.

Riverside, Silom & Lumphini (p92)

▶ Gay nightlife

Come nighttime, gay visitors and locals alike flock to the side streets off lower Th Silom. The alternatives run the gamut from seedy boy bars to sophisticated dance clubs – and just about everything in between.

Royal City Avenue (RCA) (p112)

▶ Dance clubs
▶ Live music

Hands-down the city's premier nightlife strip; RCA's clubs were formerly a teen scene, but the area has grown up in recent years and today draws a wide spectrum of partiers, not to mention

Street market, Chinatown (p62)

Th Yaowarat, Chinatown (p70)

a hearty selection of music, from live indie bands to big-name DJs.

Ari (p134)

▶ Restaurants
▶ Bars

Looking to up your Bangkok street cred? Casually drop the name Ari – an emerging suburban neighbourhood packed with buzzy local restaurants and bars – and you'll gain the respect of local hipsters and bewilder the tourists.

Other great places to experience the city like a local:

MBK Food Court (p82)

Amulet Market (p35)

Asia Herb Association (p118)

Th Bamrung Meuang (p53)

Chao Phraya Dinner Cruise (p104)

Siam Paragon Cineplex (p87)

Hualamphong Train Station (p66)

ThaiCraft Fair (p127)

Bangkok City Hall (p48)

Bangkok
Day Planner

Day One

Get up as early as you can to take the Chao Phraya Express boat north to Tha Chang to explore Ko Ratanakosin's must-see temples, **Wat Phra Kaew and Grand Palace** (p24), **Wat Pho** (p28) and **Wat Arun** (p32). For lunch, soak up the riverfront views from **Mangkud Cafe** (p140), or take the plunge into authentic Bangkok-style street food at **Pa Aew** (p37).

Refresh with a spa treatment at **Health Land** (p99), or soothe those overworked legs with a traditional Thai massage at **Ruen-Nuad Massage Studio** (p98). After freshening up, get a new perspective on Bangkok with rooftop cocktails at **Moon Bar** (p105).

For dinner, **nahm** (p101) serves what is arguably some of the best Thai food in Bangkok. If you've still got it in you, get dancing at **Tapas Room** (p105) or head over to **Telephone Pub** (p94) or any of the other bars in Bangkok's lush gaybourhood. For a night that doesn't end until the sun comes up, bang on the door at **Wong's Place** (p106).

Day Two

Take the BTS (Skytrain) to National Stadium and start your day with a visit to the popular and worthwhile museum that is **Jim Thompson's House** (p74). Afterwards, check out the latest exhibition at the **Bangkok Art & Culture Centre** (p78).

For lunch, the nearby **MBK Food Court** (p82) is a thorough and cheap introduction to Thai food. After eating, walk, or let the BTS escort you, through Bangkok's ultramodern commercial district, stopping off at linked shopping centres **MBK Center** (p86), **Gaysorn Plaza** (p87) and **Siam Square** (p87). Be sure to throw in a prayer for good luck at the **Erawan Shrine** (p78).

Come dinnertime, give your credit card a break and become acquainted with rustic Thai food at **Kai Thort Jay Kee** (p102). If it's a Friday or Saturday night, make a point of schlepping over to RCA (Royal City Avenue) and the fun clubs there such as **Cosmic Café** (p113) or **Slim/Flix** (p113). If it's a weekday, consider the stage show at **Calypso Cabaret** (p86) or live music at **Titanium** (p126).

Short on time?

We've arranged Bangkok's must-sees into these day-by-day itineraries to make sure you see the very best of the city in the time you have available.

Day Three

☀️ Take the *klorng* (canal, also spelt *khlong*) boat to Banglamphu, where you'll spend the first half of your day peeking into low-key but visit-worthy temples such as the **Golden Mount and Wat Saket** (p46) and **Wat Suthat** (p46). Swing through the artisan village that is **Ban Baat** (p46) followed by a visit to the bizarre strip of religious commerce that is **Th Bamrung Meuang** (p53).

☀️ Have lunch at equal parts homey and lauded Thai restaurant, **Krua Apsorn** (p48). Spend the afternoon along the famous backpacker destination that is Th Khao San, people-watching and picking up souvenirs at the **Th Khao San Market** (p55).

🌙 For dinner, head over to Th Sukhumvit and take a temporary break from Thai food at one of this strip's great international restaurants such **Nasir Al-Masri** (p120) or **Myeong Ga** (p120). End the night with a Thai-themed cocktail at a cosy local such as **WTF** (p123) or **Soul Food Mahanakorn** (p119), or a streetside Singha at **Cheap Charlie's** (p123). If it's still too early to head in, extend the night with dancing at **Bed Supperclub** (p123) or rooftop drinks at **Nest** (p124).

Day Four

☀️ If it's a weekend, take the BTS north for a half-day of shopping at the **Chatuchak Weekend Market** (p130). Otherwise, consider a half-day excursion outside the city to the artificial island of **Ko Kret** (p136).

☀️ Take time to recover from the market (or your excursion), and in the relative cool of the late afternoon take the MRT (metro) to Chinatown and visit the home of the Golden Buddha, **Wat Traimit** (p60), and the Chinese-style **Wat Mangkon Kamalawat** (p65). Consider popping over to **Phahurat** (p66) to sample that neighbourhood's South Asian feel. For dinner, try our food-based **walking tour** (p62) of Chinatown's famous street stalls.

🌙 After dinner, consider heading to **Pak Khlong Talat** (p65), Bangkok's nocturnal flower market. Alternatively, cross to Banglamphu and kick the night off with drinks at **Hippie de Bar** (p52), followed by a rowdy live-music show at **Brick Bar** (p53). If bedtime is irrelevant, head up to upstairs to the *sheeshas* (water pipes) and dance floor of **Gazebo** (p43).

Need to Know

For more information, see Survival Guide (p161)

Currency
Thai baht (B)

Language
Thai

Visas
International air arrivals receive a 30-day visa; 60-day visas are available from a Thai consulate before leaving home.

Money
ATMs are widespread and charge a 150B foreign-account fee. Visa and MasterCard are accepted at upmarket places.

Mobile Phones
Thailand is on a GSM and 3G network through inexpensive pre-paid SIM cards.

Time
Asia/Bangkok (GMT/UTC plus seven hours).

Plugs & Adaptors
Plugs have two-prong round or flat sockets; electrical current is 220V.

Tipping
Tipping is generally not expected in Thailand.

① Before You Go

Your Daily Budget

Budget less than 1500B
▶ Dorm bed/basic guesthouse room 160B–800B

▶ Street-stall meals

▶ A couple of the big-hitter sights, supplemented with free temples and parks

Midrange 1500B–3000B
▶ Flashpacker guesthouse or midrange hotel room 800B–1500B

▶ Shophouse restaurant meals

▶ Most, if not all, of the big sights

Top End more than 3000B
▶ Boutique hotel room 3000B

▶ Fine dining

▶ Private tours

Websites

Lonely Planet (www.lonelyplanet.com/bangkok) Info, hotel bookings and more.

BK (www.bk.asia-city.com) Online version of Bangkok's best listings magazine.

Bangkok 101 (www.bangkok101.com) Tourist-friendly listings mag.

Advance Planning

Three months before Book at a boutique hotel, especially for December/January.

One month before Apply for a visa at the Thai embassy or consulate in your home country if you plan to stay longer than 30 days; make reservations at nahm.

A week before Buy clothes appropriate for hot weather; book lessons at a Thai cooking school.

② Arriving in Bangkok

Suvarnabhumi is Bangkok's primary international air hub and is located 25km east of the city centre. Don Muang, Bangkok's low-cost terminal, is north of the city.

✈ From Suvarnabhumi International Airport (BKK)

Destination	Best Transport
Banglamphu, Ko Ratanakosin & Thonburi	taxi, bus 556
Chinatown	Airport Link (transfer to MRT), taxi
Siam Square	Airport Link (transfer to BTS), taxi
Riverside, Silom & Lumphini	Airport Link (transfer to MRT or BTS), taxi

✈ From Don Muang Airport (DMK)

Destination	Best Transport
Banglamphu, Ko Ratanakosin & Thonburi	taxi, bus 59
Chinatown	taxi, bus 29, train
Siam Square	taxi
Riverside, Silom & Lumphini	taxi

③ Getting Around

Bangkok's public transportation network is continually growing, but it is still only relatively expansive, and getting to certain parts of the city – particularly the older areas – remains extremely time-consuming. The best strategy is usually to combine a longer trip on the BTS or MRT with a short taxi ride.

S BTS

The elevated Skytrain (www.bts.co.th) is probably the most efficient and convenient way to get around central Bangkok.

M MRT

Bangkok's metro (www.metro.co.th) is also convenient, although not quite as expansive as the BTS.

🚕 Taxi

Outside peak hours, Bangkok taxis are a great bargain.

⚓ Chao Phraya River Express

These boats (www.chaophrayaexpressboat .com.th) are a slow but steady way to visit the tourist sights along the Chao Phraya River.

⚓ Klorng Boat

Bangkok's canal boats are generally more useful for commuters than visitors.

🚌 Bus

Bangkok's buses (www.bmta.co.th) are a cheap but slow and confusing way to get around the city.

Bangkok
Neighbourhoods

Banglamphu (p40)
Despite being home to the intergalactic melting pot that is Th Khao San, this district of antique shophouses and temples remains the city's most characteristically 'Bangkok' neighbourhood.

Dusit Palace Park

Ko Ratanakosin & Thonburi (p22)
Bangkok's riverside historical centre includes the monuments to king, country and religion that draw most tourists.

👁 **Top Sights**

Wat Phra Kaew & Grand Palace

Wat Pho

Wat Arun

Wat Phra Kaew & Grand Palace

Jim Thompson's House

Wat Pho

Wat Arun

Wat Traimit (Golden Buddha)

Chinatown (p58)
Home to shark-fin restaurants, gaudy gold and jade shops and flashing neon signs in Chinese characters, Chinatown is Bangkok's most hectic neighbourhood.

👁 **Top Sights**

Wat Traimit (Golden Buddha)

Chatuchak Weekend Market 👁

Siam Square, Pratunam & Ploenchit (p72)

The area around Siam Square is essentially one giant shopping mall, and today is considered the unofficial centre of modern Bangkok.

👁 **Top Sights**

Jim Thompson's House

Worth a Trip

👁 **Top Sights**

Chatuchak Weekend Market

Dusit Palace Park

Ko Kret

Thanon Sukhumvit (p114)

Dominating the area east of central Bangkok is Th Sukhumvit, a busy commercial and residential neighbourhood with modern midrange hotels, which is a favourite of expatriates and cosmopolitan Thais.

Riverside, Silom & Lumphini (p92)

This is Bangkok's de facto financial district, and most locals come here to work, while you'll probably come to eat, play or stay.

Explore

Bangkok

Worth a Trip

Street food, Chinatown (p62)
KYLIE MCLAUGHLIN/GETTY IMAGES ©

Explore

Ko Ratanakosin & Thonburi

The artificial island of Ko Ratanakosin is Bangkok's birthplace, and the Buddhist temples and royal palaces here comprise some of the city's most important and most visited sights. By contrast, Thonburi, located across Mae Nam Chao Phraya (Chao Phraya River), is a seemingly forgotten yet visit-worthy zone of sleepy residential districts connected by *klorng* (canals, also spelt *khlong*).

The Sights in a Day

Get an early start – to take advantage of the cool weather and beat the crowds – and begin your day at what is arguably Bangkok's premier sight, **Wat Phra Kaew and Grand Palace** (p24). Make the short walk next door and feel your jaw dropping to the floor at the sight of the immense reclining Buddha at **Wat Pho** (p28).

You're going to be tired, hungry and hot at this point, so recharge at the generously air-conditioned restaurant **Coconut Palm** (p37). After lunch, stop in for a massage at the **Wat Pho Thai Traditional Medical and Massage School** (p35) or, if intellectual rather than physical stimulation is your thing, investigate the fun exhibits at the **Museum of Siam** (p35) or the ancient treasures at the **National Museum** (p35).

Come late afternoon, cross Mae Nam Chao Phraya and climb around on **Wat Arun** (p32). Coordinate your return to Ko Ratanakosin with sunset and cocktails at **Amorosa** (p39). Cross the river yet again for dinner at **Mangkud Cafe** (p37), or make the short walk to **Khunkung** (p37).

⊙ Top Sights

Wat Phra Kaew & Grand Palace (p24)

Wat Pho (p28)

Wat Arun (p32)

♥ Best of Bangkok

Temples

Wat Phra Kaew & Grand Palace (p24)

Wat Pho (p28)

Wat Arun (p32)

Museums

Museum of Siam (p35)

National Museum (p35)

Songkran Niyomsane Forensic Medicine Museum & Parasite Museum (p35)

Massage

Wat Pho Thai Traditional Medical & Massage School (p35)

Getting There

River ferry To Ko Ratanakosin: Tha Tien and Tha Chang. To Thonburi: Tha Wang Lang (Siriraj) and Tha Saphan Phra Pin Klao.

S BTS To Thonburi: Krung Thonburi or Wong Wian Yai and taxi

Top Sights
Wat Phra Kaew & Grand Palace

Also known as the Temple of the Emerald Buddha, Wat Phra Kaew is the colloquial name of the vast, fairy-tale compound that also includes the former residence of the Thai monarch, the Grand Palace. The ground was consecrated in 1782, the first year of Bangkok rule, and is today Bangkok's biggest tourist attraction and a pilgrimage destination for devout Buddhists and nationalists. Today, the 94.5-hectare grounds encompass more than 100 buildings that represent 200 years of royal history and architectural experimentation.

วัดพระแก้ว/พระบรม
มหาราชวัง

◉ Map p34, C4

Th Na Phra Lan

admission 400B

⏱8.30am-3.30pm

🚢Tha Chang

Mythical creatures guarding Wat Phra Kaew

Don't Miss

The Emerald Buddha

On a tall platform in Wat Phra Kaew's fantastically decorated *bòht* (main chapel), the Emerald Buddha is the temple's primary attraction. Despite the name, the statue is actually carved from a single piece of nephrite, a type of jade. The diminutive figure (it's only 66cm tall) is always cloaked in royal robes, one for each season (hot, cool and rainy).

Some time in the 15th century, the Emerald Buddha is said to have been covered with plaster and gold leaf and placed in Chiang Rai's own Wat Phra Kaew. Many valuable Buddha images were masked in this way to deter potential thieves and marauders during unstable times. Often the true identity of the image was forgotten over the years until a 'divine accident' exposed its precious core. The Emerald Buddha experienced such a divine revelation while it was being transported to a new location. In a fall, the plaster covering broke off, revealing the brilliant green inside.

Later, during territorial clashes with Laos during the mid-16th century, the Emerald Buddha was seized and taken to modern-day Laos. Some 200 years later, the Thai army marched up to Vientiane, razed the city and hauled off the Emerald Buddha. The Buddha was enshrined in the then capital, Thonburi, before the general who led the sacking of Vientiane assumed the throne and had it moved to its present location.

Ramakian Murals

Recently restored murals of the *Ramakian* (the Thai version of the Indian epic the Ramayana) line the inside walls of the Wat Phra Kaew compound. Originally painted during the reign of Rama I (King Phraphutthayotfa; r 1782–1809),

☑ Top Tips

▶ Enter Wat Phra Kaew and the Grand Palace complex through the clearly marked third gate from the river pier. Tickets are purchased inside the complex; anyone telling you it's closed is a gem tout or con artist.

▶ At Wat Phra Kaew and the Grand Palace grounds, dress rules are strictly enforced. If you're flashing a bit too much skin, expect to be shown into a dressing room and issued with a shirt or sarong (rental is free, but you must provide a 200B deposit).

▶ Admission for the complex includes entrance to Dusit Palace Park (p56).

✗ Take a Break

There isn't much in the way of interesting eating or drinking in the immediate area. Your best bet is probably to hop on the 3B river-crossing ferry at Tha Chang and grab a bite at Mangkud Cafe (p37).

the 178 sections illustrate the epic in its entirety, beginning at the north gate and moving clockwise around the compound.

Guardians of Wat Phra Kaew

The first sights you'll see upon entering Wat Phra Kaew are two 5m-high *yaksha*, giants or ogres with origins in Hindu/Buddhist mythology. Other mythical creatures in the temple compound include the half-human, half-bird *kinnaree* and the sacred birds known as garuda, not to mention various hermits and elephants.

Phra Mondop

Commissioned by Rama I, this structure was built for the storage of sacred Buddhist manuscripts, and the seven-tiered roof, floor woven from strands of silver and intricate mother-of-pearl door panels make it among the most decadent libraries we've encountered. Phra Mondop is closed to the public.

Chakri Mahaprasat

The largest of the Grand Palace buildings is the Chakri Mahaprasat (Grand Palace Hall). Completed in 1882 following a plan by British architects, the exterior shows a blend of Italian Renaissance and traditional Thai architecture. The central spire contains the ashes of Chakri kings; the flanking spires enshrine the ashes of the Chakri princes who failed to inherit the throne.

Amarindra Hall

Originally a hall of justice, this large, mostly empty hall is used for coronation ceremonies – the most recent occasion being the current king's coronation in 1950. The golden, boat-shaped throne looks considerably more ornate than comfortable.

Borombhiman Hall

This French-inspired structure served as a residence for Rama VI (King Vajiravudh; r 1910–25). The palace was where Rama VIII (King Ananda Mahidol; r 1935–46) was mysteriously murdered in 1946, and in April 1981 General San Chitpatima used it as the headquarters for an attempted coup. Today the structure can only be viewed through its iron gates.

Dusit Hall

The compound's westernmost structure is the Ratanakosin-style Dusit Hall, which initially served as a venue for royal audiences and later as a royal funerary hall.

Wat Phra Kaew & The Grand Palace

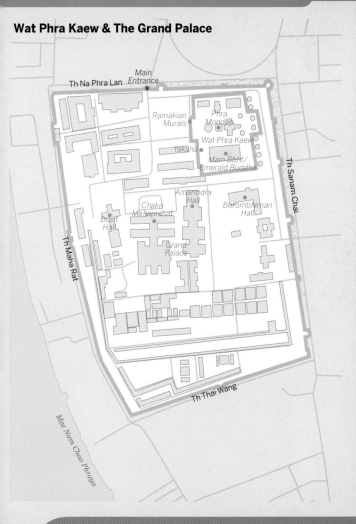

Top Sights
Wat Pho

Of all Bangkok's temples, Wat Pho is arguably the one most worth visiting for both its remarkable reclining Buddha image and its sprawling, stupa-studded grounds. The compound boasts a long list of credits: the oldest and largest wát in Bangkok; the longest reclining Buddha; the largest collection of Buddha images in Thailand; and the country's first public education institution. For all that, it sees fewer visitors than neighbouring Wat Phra Kaew and feels less commercial.

วัดโพธิ์ (วัดพระเชตุพน), Wat Phra Chetuphon

👁 Map p34, D5

Th Sanam Chai

admission 100B

🕑 8.30am-6.30pm

🚢 Tha Tien

Reclining Buddha, Wat Pho

Don't Miss

Reclining Buddha

Located in the main *wí·hǎhn* (sanctuary), the genuinely impressive Reclining Buddha, 46m long and 15m high, illustrates the passing of the Buddha into nirvana (ie the Buddha's death). The figure is modelled out of plaster around a brick core and finished in gold leaf. Mother-of-pearl inlay ornaments the feet, displaying the 108 different auspicious *lák·sà·nà* (characteristics) of a Buddha. Continuing the theme, alongside the statue are 108 bronze monk bowls; for 20B you can buy 108 coins, each of which is dropped in a bowl for good luck.

Massage

At what other sacred religious sight in the world can you get a massage? Wat Pho is the national headquarters for the teaching of traditional Thai medicine, which includes Thai massage. The famous massage school has two **massage pavilions** (Thai massage per hr 420B; ⏰8.30am-6.30pm) located within the temple compound and additional rooms within a training facility outside the temple.

Phra Ubosot

Though built during the reign of Rama I, the *ubosot* (chapel) as it stands today is the result of renovations dating back to the reign of Rama III (King Phranangklao; r 1824–51). Inside you'll find impressive murals and a three-tiered pedestal supporting Phra Buddha Deva Patimakorn, the compound's second-most noteworthy Buddha statue, as well as the ashes of Rama I.

Other Buddha Statues

The images on display in the four *wí·hǎhn* (sanctuaries) surrounding the Phra Ubosot are worth

☑ Top Tips

▶ Arrive early to avoid the crowds and take advantage of the (relatively) cool weather.

▶ If you're hot and footsore, the air-conditioned massage pavilions near Wat Pho's east gate could be a welcome way to cool down while experiencing high-quality and relatively inexpensive Thai massage.

▶ A donation of 20B gets you 108 tiny coins, which you can drop into the 108 bowls lined up in the main *bòht* – the number 108 being important in Hindu and Buddhist belief, and the act regarded as auspicious among Thais.

✖ Take a Break

Convenient and delicious refreshment after your temple visit (or massage) can be obtained at retro-themed Rub Aroon Cafe (p39) or graciously air-conditioned Coconut Palm (p37).

investigation. Particularly beautiful are the Phra Jinnarat and Phra Jinachi Buddhas in the western and southern *wí·hǎhn*, both rescued from Sukhothai by relatives of Rama I. The galleries extending between the four structures feature no fewer than 394 gilded Buddha images.

Ancient Inscriptions
Encircling the Phra Ubosot is a low marble wall with 152 bas-reliefs depicting scenes from the Ramakian. You'll recognise some of these figures when you exit the temple past the hawkers with mass-produced rubbings for sale; these are made from cement casts based on Wat Pho's reliefs. Nearby, a small pavilion has Unesco-recognised inscriptions detailing the tenets of traditional Thai massage.

Stupas
On the western side of the grounds a collection of four towering stupas commemorates the first four Chakri kings. Note the square bell shape with distinct corners, a signature of Ratanakosin style, and the tiles emulating the colours of the Buddhist flag. Wat Pho's 91 smaller stupas include *chedi* (stupa) clusters containing the ashes of lesser royal descendants.

Phra Mondop
Also known as *hǒr đrai*, and serving as a depository for Buddhist scriptures, the elevated Phra Mondop is guarded by four *yaksha*, or giants.

Wat Pho

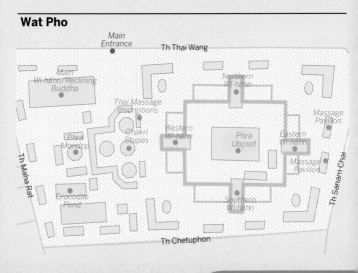

Understand
Wat Pho's Rock Giants

Aside from monks and sightseers, Wat Pho is filled with an altogether stiffer crowd: dozens of giants and figurines carved from granite. The rock giants first arrived in Thailand as ballast aboard Chinese junks and were put to work in Wat Pho (and other wát, including Wat Suthat, p46), guarding the entrances of temple gates and courtyards. Look closely and you'll see an array of Chinese characters. The giants with bulging eyes and Chinese opera costumes were inspired by warrior noblemen and are called Lan Than. The figure in a straw hat is a farmer, forever interrupted during his day's work cultivating the fields. And can you recognise the guy in the fedora-like hat with a trimmed beard and moustache? Marco Polo, of course, who introduced such European styles to the Chinese court.

Legend has it that an argument between the four (over money, of course) led to the clearing of the area known today as Tha Tien. Just south of Phra Mondop is the currently reptile-free Crocodile Pond.

The Grounds
Small Chinese-style rock gardens and hill islands interrupt the tiled courtyards, providing shade, greenery and quirky decorations depicting daily life. Keep an eye out for the distinctive rockery festooned with figures of the hermit Khao Mor, who is credited with inventing yoga, in various healing positions. According to the tradition, a few good arm stretches should cure idleness.

Top Sights
Wat Arun

The missile-shaped temple that rises from the banks of Mae Nam Chao Phraya is known as Temple of Dawn, and was named after the Indian god of dawn, Aruna. It was here that King Taksin stumbled upon a shrine and interpreted the discovery as such an auspicious sign that this should be the site of the new capital of Siam. Today, Wat Arun is known for its emblematic spire, and is one of the few Buddhist temples visitors can climb on.

วัดอรุณฯ

👁 Map p34, B5

www.watarun.net

off Th Arun Amarin

admission 50B

🕗8am-6pm

🚤Tha Tien

Wat Arun, on the banks of Mae Nam Chao Phraya

Don't Miss

The Spire

The central feature of Wat Arun is the 82m-high Khmer-style *brahng* (spire), constructed during the first half of the 19th century. From the river it is not apparent that this steeple is adorned with colourful floral murals made of glazed porcelain, a common temple ornamentation in the early Ratanakosin period, when Chinese ships calling at Bangkok used the stuff as ballast.

The Main Chapel

The *bòht*, or main chapel, contains a Buddha image that is said to have been designed by Rama II (King Phraphutthaloetla Naphalai; r 1809–24) himself, as well as beautiful murals that depict Prince Siddhartha (the Buddha) encountering examples of birth, old age, sickness and death outside his palace walls, an experience that led him to abandon the worldly life.

The Grounds

In addition to the central spire and main chapel, the Wat Arun compound includes two *wí·hăhn* (sanctuaries) and a *hŏr drai* (a depository for Buddhist scripture), among others. Adjacent to the river are six Chinese-style *săh·lah* (often spelt as *sala*), open-air pavilions traditionally meant for relaxing or study, but increasingly used these days as docks for tourist boats.

Exploring the Neighbourhood

Many people visit Wat Arun on long-tail boat tours, but it's dead easy and more rewarding to just jump on the 3B cross-river ferry from Tha Tien. Once there, consider taking a stroll away from the river on Th Wang Doem, a quiet tiled street of wooden shophouses.

☑ **Top Tips**

▸ You must wear appropriate clothing to climb on Wat Arun. If you are flashing too much flesh, you'll have to rent a sarong for 20B.

▸ For our money, it's best to visit Wat Arun in the late afternoon, when the sun shines from the west, lighting up the spire and the river behind it.

▸ Sunset views of the temple compound can be caught from across the river at the riverfront warehouses that line Th Maha Rat – although be forewarned that locals may ask for a 20B 'fee'.

✗ **Take a Break**

If you're visiting Wat Arun at sunset, a great place to soak up the views is Amorosa (p39), the rooftop bar at the Arun Residence.

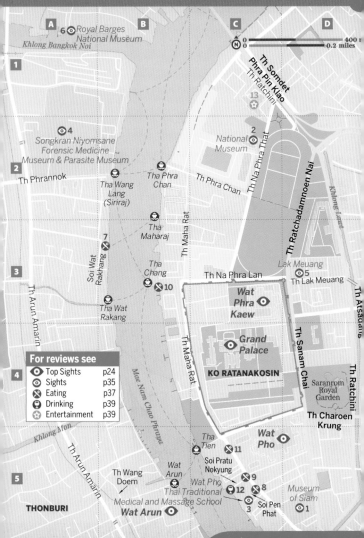

Royal Barges
National Museum
6
A
B
C
D
N
0   400 r
0   0.2 miles

Khlong Bangkok Noi

Th Somdet
Phra Pin Klao
Th Ratchini

13

1

4
Songkran Niyomsane
Forensic Medicine
Museum & Parasite Museum

*National
Museum*
2

Th Na Phra That

2

Th Phrannok

*Tha Wang
Lang
(Siriraj)*

*Tha Phra
Chan*

Th Phra Chan

Th Ratchadamnoen Nai

Khlong Lawt

*Tha
Maharaj*

Th Maha Rat

7

Soi Wat
Rakhang

*Tha
Chang*

10

Lak Meuang
5
Th Lak Meuang

3

Th Arun Amarin

*Tha Wat
Rakang*

Th Na Phra Lan

*Wat
Phra
Kaew*

Th Sanam Chai

Th Atsadang

Th Ratchini

*Grand
Palace*

KO RATANAKOSIN

*Saranrom
Royal
Garden*

For reviews see

	Top Sights	p24
	Sights	p35
	Eating	p37
	Drinking	p39
	Entertainment	p39

4

Mae Nam Chao Phraya

Th Charoen
Krung

Khlong Mon

Th Arun Amarin

*Tha
Tien*

*Wat
Pho*

11

Soi Pratu
Nokyung

9

*Museum
of Siam*

5

Th Wang
Doem

*Wat
Arun*

*Wat Pho
Thai Traditional
Medical and Massage School*

12

8

Soi Pen
Phat

1

THONBURI

Wat Arun

3

Sights

Museum of Siam · MUSEUM

1 · Map p34, D5

This fun museum employs a variety of methods and media to explore the origins of the Thai people and their culture. Housed in a European-style 19th-century building that was once the Ministry of Commerce, the exhibits are presented in an engaging, interactive fashion not often found in Thailand. A great option for those travelling with kids. (สถาบันพิพิธภัณฑ์การเรียนรู้แห่งชาติ; www.museumsiam.com; Th Maha Rat; admission 300B; ⏰10am-6pm Tue-Sun; 🚤Tha Tien)

National Museum · MUSEUM

2 · Map p34, C2

Thailand's National Museum is the largest in Southeast Asia and covers a broad range of subjects, from historical surveys to religious sculpture displays. The buildings were originally constructed in 1782 as the palace of Rama I's viceroy, Prince Wang Na. Rama V (King Chulalongkorn; r 1868–1910) turned it into a museum in 1884. Free guided tours are given on Wednesday and Thursday at 9.30am. (พิพิธภัณฑสถานแห่งชาติ; 4 Th Na Phra That; admission 200B; ⏰9am-3.30pm Wed-Sun; 🚤Tha Chang)

Wat Pho Thai Traditional Medical & Massage School · MASSAGE

3 · Map p34, C5

Stop by for a massage (per hour 420B), or if you've got more time, enrol in one of several reputable massage courses. The school is outside the temple compound in a restored Bangkok shophouse at the end of unmarked Soi Pen Phat; look for Coconut Palm restaurant. (📞0 2622 3551; www.watpomassage.com; 392/25-28 Soi Pen Phat; tuition from 9500B; ⏰8am-6pm; 🚤Tha Tien)

Songkran Niyomsane Forensic Medicine Museum & Parasite Museum · MUSEUM

4 · Map p34, A2

While it's not exactly CSI, pickled body parts, ingenious murder weapons and other crime-scene evidence are on

Local Life
Amulet Market

Bangkok's arcane and fascinating **amulet market** (Map p34, B2; ตลาดพระเครื่องวัดมหาธาตุ; Th Maha Rat; ⏰7am-5pm; 🚤Tha Chang) claims the footpaths along Th Maha Rat and Th Phra Chan, as well as a dense network of covered market stalls near Tha Phra Chan. The trade is based around small talismans highly prized by collectors, monks, taxi drivers and people in dangerous professions.

Monks at the amulet market (p35)

display at this medical museum. Next door, the Parasite Museum continues the queasy theme. The best way to get here is by express ferry or cross-river ferry to Tha Wang Lang (Siriraj) in Thonburi; turn right (north) into the hospital and follow the green 'Museum' signs. (พิพิธภัณฑ์นิติเวชศาสตร์สงกรานต์นิยมเสน; 2nd fl, Adulyadejvikrom Bldg, Siriraj Hospital; admission 40B; ⏲9am-4pm Mon-Sat; 🚢Tha Wang Lang (Siriraj))

Lak Meuang   ANIMIST SHRINE

5 ◉ Map p34, D3

Lak Meuang is Bangkok's city shrine, a wooden pillar erected by Rama I in 1782 to represent the founding of the new capital. Like other sacred shrines in Thailand, Lak Meuang receives daily invocations from worshippers in the form of commissioned *lá·kon gâa bon* (a traditional dance) as thanks for granted wishes. (ศาลหลักเมือง; cnr Th Sanam Chai & Th Lak Meuang; admission free; ⏲6.30am-6.30pm; 🚢Tha Chang)

Royal Barges National Museum   MUSEUM

6 ◉ Map p34, A1

For ceremonial occasions, the elaborately carved barges here are dusted off for a grand riverine procession. The Supphannahong boat traditionally carries the king and is the world's largest dugout. Visit the museum as part of the longtail boat tour of Thonburi, or from Tha Saphan Pin Klao, turn down Th Somdet Phra Pin Klao 1 and follow the signs. (เรือพระที่นั่ง; Khlong Bangkok Noi or 80/1 Th Arun Amarin; admission 100B,

camera/video 100/200B; ⏱9am-5pm; 🛥Tha
Saphan Phra Pin Klao)

Eating

Mangkud Cafe
CENTRAL THAI $

7 🍴 Map p34, B3

Combining a warehouse-like art gallery and a minimalist dining room,
Mangkud is probably the most sophisticated place to eat on this side of Mae
Nam Chao Phraya. The river views
are unparalleled, and the upscale-ish
herb-heavy Thai dishes are clever
and tasty; try the watermelon with
dried fish, a traditional sweet-savoury
snack. Look for the sign that says Club
Arts. (Club Arts; www.clubartsgallery.com; Soi
Wat Rakhang; mains 125-300B; ⏱10.30am-
11pm Tue-Thu, to midnight Fri-Sun; 📶; 🛥from
Tha Chang)

Coconut Palm
CENTRAL THAI $

8 🍴 Map p34, C5

Coconut Palm serves a generous
spread of Thai dishes, but most locals

come for the Sukhothai-style noodles:
thin rice noodles served with pork,
ground peanuts and dried chilli. Even
if you're not hungry, you might want
to stop by for the reinvigorating blast
of air-con and the refreshing drinks.
(392/1-2 Th Maha Rat; mains 40-100B;
⏱11am-6pm; ❄ 📶; 🛥Tha Tien)

Pa Aew
CENTRAL THAI $

9 🍴 Map p34, C5

Yes, it's a bare-bones open-air curry
stall, but if we're talking taste, Pa Aew
is our favourite place to eat in this
part of town. Pull up a plastic stool
for rich, seafood-heavy Bangkok-style
dishes. Pa Aew is located near the
corner with Soi Pratu Nokyung; look
for the exposed trays of dishes in front
of Krung Thai Bank. (Th Maha Rat; mains
20-60B; ⏱10am-5pm; 🛥Tha Tien)

Khunkung
THAI $$

10 🍴 Map p34, B3

The restaurant of the Royal Navy
Association has one of the coveted
riverfront locations along this stretch

⊙ Local Life
Exploring Thonburi's Canals

For an up-close view of Thonburi's famed canals, long-tail boats are avail-
able for charter at Tha Chang and Tha Tien. Trips explore the canals **Khlong
Bangkok Noi** and **Khlong Bangkok Yai**, taking in the Royal Barges National
Museum, Wat Arun and a riverside temple with fish feeding. Longer trips
diverge into **Khlong Mon**, between Bangkok Noi and Bangkok Yai. However,
it's worth pointing out that the most common tour of one hour (1000B, up to
six people) does not allow you enough time to disembark and explore any of
these sights. To do so, you'll need 1½ hours (1300B) or two hours (1600B).

Understand
What's a Wát?

Bangkok is home to hundreds of wáts, temple compounds that have traditionally been at the centre of community life.

Buildings & Structures
Even the smallest wát will usually have a *bòht, wí·hǎhn* and monks' living quarters.

▶ **Bòht** The most sacred prayer room at a wát, often similar in size and shape to the *wí·hǎhn*. Aside from the fact it does not house the main Buddha image, you'll know the *bòht* because it is usually more ornately decorated and has eight cornerstones to ward off evil.

▶ **Chedi (stupa)** A large bell-shaped tower usually containing five structural elements symbolising (from bottom to top) earth, water, fire, wind and void; depending on the wát, relics of the Buddha, a Thai king or some other notable are housed inside.

▶ **Drum Tower** Elevates the ceremonial drum beaten by novices.

▶ **Mon·dòp** An open-sided, square building with four arches and a pyramidal roof; used to worship religious objects or texts.

▶ **Hǒr drai** The manuscript library: a structure for holding Buddhist scriptures. As these texts were previously made from palm leaves, *hǒr drai* were typically elevated or built over water to protect texts from flooding and/or termites.

▶ **Prang** A towering phallic spire of Khmer origin serving the same religious purpose as a *chedi*.

▶ **Sǎh·lah (sala)** A pavilion, often open-sided, for relaxation or lessons.

▶ **Wí·hǎhn (vihara)** The sanctuary for the temple's main Buddha image and where laypeople come to make their offerings. Classic architecture typically has a three-tiered roof representing the triple gems: the Buddha (the teacher), Dharma (the teaching) and Brotherhood (the followers).

of the Mae Nam Chao Phraya. Locals come for the combination of river views and cheap and tasty seafood-based eats – not for the cafeteria-like atmosphere. The entrance to the restaurant is near the ATM machines at Tha Chang. (Navy Club; 77 Th Maha Rat; mains 75-720B; ⏰11am-2pm & 6-10pm Mon-Fri, 11am-10pm Sat & Sun; ❋📱; 🚤Tha Chang)

Rub Aroon Cafe THAI $

11 🍴 Map p34, C5

This traveller-friendly cafe is a pleasant escape from sightseeing in Ko Ratanakosin. The restored shopfront opens directly out to the street with cosy seating and patient service. The dishes are basic and satisfying, served alongside fruit drinks and coffees for sipping away tropical fatigue. (Th Maha Rat; mains 75-120B; ⏰8am-6pm; 📱; 🚤Tha Tien)

Drinking

Amorosa BAR

12 🍷 Map p34, C5

Perched above the Arun Residence, Amorosa takes advantage of a location directly above the river and opposite Wat Arun. The cocktails aren't going to blow you away, but watching boats ply their way along the royal river as Wat Arun is lit up behind is a stark and beautiful reminder that you're not home anymore. (www.arunresidence.com; rooftop, Arun Residence, 36-38 Soi Pratu

Nokyung; ⏰5pm-midnight Mon-Thu, to 1am Fri-Sun; 🚤Tha Tien)

Entertainment

National Theatre THEATRE

13 ⭐ Map p34, C1

After a lengthy renovation, the National Theatre is again open for business. Performances of *kŏhn*, masked dance-drama often depicting scenes from the Ramayana, are held on the first and second Sundays of the month; *lá·kon*, Thai dance-dramas, are held on the last Friday of the month; and Thai musical performances are held on the third Friday of the month. (📞0 2224 1342; 2 Th Ratchini; tickets 60-100B; 🚤Tha Chang)

✅ Top Tip

Dress for Success

Most of Bangkok's biggest tourist attractions are in fact sacred places, and visitors should dress and behave appropriately. In particular, at Wat Phra Kaew & Grand Palace, you won't be allowed to enter unless you're well covered. Shorts, sleeveless shirts or spaghetti-strap tops, capri pants – basically anything that reveals more than your arms (not your shoulders) and head – are not allowed. Those who aren't dressed appropriately can expect to be shown into a dressing room and issued with a sarong before being allowed in.

Explore

Banglamphu

Leafy lanes, antique shophouses, buzzing wet markets and golden temples convene in Banglamphu – easily the city's most quintessentially 'Bangkok' neighbourhood. It's a quaint postcard picture of the city that used to be – that is until you stumble upon Th Khao San, the intergalactic backpacker melting pot that's anything but traditional.

The Sights in a Day

☀️ Start your day with a bird's-eye view of Banglamphu from the peak of the **Golden Mount** (p46). Descend and learn about the unique local trade at nearby **Ban Baat** (p46). Continue by foot to the impressive but little-visited **Wat Suthat** (p46).

☀️ You're now a short walk from classic Bangkok-style restaurants **Poj Spa Kar** (p50) and **Chote Chitr** (p51). After refuelling, cross over to Th Khao San, taking in the famous backpacker district's hectic **street market** (p55). Indulge in even more retail at niche shops **Nittaya Curry Shop** (p55) or **Taekee Taekon** (p55), or relax by the river at **Phra Sumen Fort & Santichaiprakan Park** (p47).

🌙 Come evening, you have two options. If you're more of a spectator, consider an **Isan-style dinner** (p51) followed by a few rounds of Thai boxing at **Ratchadamnoen Stadium** (p53); if you've got partying on the mind, hit the decadent noodles at **Jay Fai** (p48) followed by a drinks with local hipsters at **Hippie de Bar** (p52) or **Taksura** (p52).

For a local's night out in Banglamphu, see p42.

🔍 **Local Life**

Banglamphu Pub Crawl (p42)

💜 **Best of Bangkok**

Temples
Golden Mount & Wat Saket (p46)

Wat Suthat (p46)

Wat Bowonniwet (p47)

Live Music
Brick Bar (p53)

Ad Here the 13th (p55)

Eating
Krua Apsorn (p48)

Jay Fai (p48)

Shopping
Th Khao San Market (p55)

Drinking
Hippie de Bar (p52)

Getting There

🚢 **River ferry** Tha Phra Athit (Banglamphu)

🚢 **Klorng boat** Tha Phan Fah

Local Life
Banglamphu Pub Crawl

You don't need to go far to find a decent bar in Banglamphu – it's one of Bangkok's best nightlife 'hoods. But why limit yourself to one? With this in mind, we've assembled a pub crawl that spans river views, people-watching, live music and late-night shenanigans.

❶ River Views
Start your crawl with sunset drinks along Th Phra Athit. To take advantage of the river views try **Phra Arthit River Lounge** (📞0 2282 9202; 23 Th Phra Athit; 🕑2pm-midnight; 🚤Tha Phra Athit (Banglamphu)), a rustic bar with tasty Thai-inspired cocktails.

❷ People-Watching
Cross over to Soi Ram Buttri for phase two of your crawl. **Gecko Bar**

(cnr Soi Chana Songkhram & Soi Rambutri; ⏰6pm-1am) is a fun and frugal place to gawk at passersby, while a few doors down, **Madame Musur** (41 Soi Ram Buttri; ⏰8am-1am; 🚤Tha Phra Athit (Banglamphu)) offers the same perks, but with a bit more sophistication and northern-style Thai dishes.

❸ Urban Beach

There's seems to be a current and inexplicable trend for beach-themed, almost tiki bar-feeling pubs in Banglamphu. If this appeals, head south on Soi Ram Buttri and hunker down with a fruity cocktail among the Easter Island heads and bamboo decor of **Sawasdee House** (Soi Ram Buttri; ⏰11am-2am; 🚤Tha Phra Athit (Banglamphu)) or, just south of Th Chakraphong, **Macaroni Club** (Th Rambuttri; ⏰24hr; 🚤Tha Phra Athit (Banglamphu)).

❹ Live Music

Every pub crawl needs a cheesy covers soundtrack (if you haven't yet heard a live version of 'Hotel California', you haven't really been to Bangkok), so continue along Th Rambuttri stopping in at the numerous open-air live-music bars such as **Barlamphu** (Th Rambuttri; ⏰noon-2am; 🚤Tha Phra Athit (Banglamphu)) or, 150m further south along Th Rambuttri, **Molly Bar** (108 Th Rambuttri; ⏰8pm-1am; 🚤Tha Phra Athit (Banglamphu)).

❺ Th Khao San

At this point, you should be sufficiently lubricated for the main event: Th Khao San. Get a bird's-eye view of the multinational backpacker parade from elevated **Roof Bar** (Th Khao San; ⏰5pm-midnight; 🚤Tha Phra Athit (Banglamphu)) or from street level at the noisy and buzzy **Center Khao Sarn** (Th Khao San; ⏰24hr; 🚤Tha Phra Athit (Banglamphu)), roughly across the street from Roof Bar.

❻ Dance Fever

If you can muster the energy, it's probably the right time to hit one of Th Khao San's nightclubs such as the dancehall-like **Club** (www.theclubkhaosan .com; 123 Th Khao San; admission free; 🚤Tha Phra Athit (Banglamphu)). Don't bother checking in before midnight.

❼ Late Night

We're guessing that 2am (closing time of most bars in the area) is probably too early to call it a night, so crawl over to **Gazebo** (www.gazebobkk.com; 3rd fl, 44 Th Chakraphong; admission 300B; ⏰6pm-late; 🚤Tha Phra Athit (Banglamphu)), a rooftop lounge and nightclub that stays open as late as you're there. Don't say we didn't warn you...

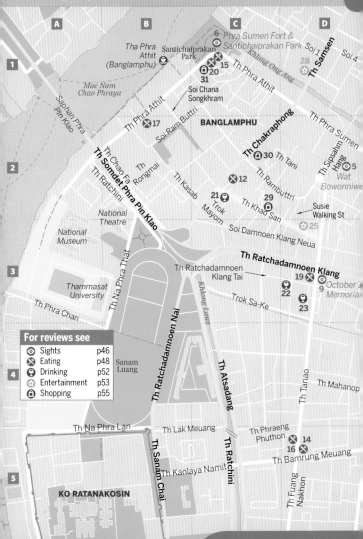

For reviews see

E F G H

1

Th Wisut Kaset

Th Krung Kasem

Khlong Phadung Kasem

Th Prachathipatai

2

24 🍴

X 18

⭐ 26

ℹ Tourism
Authority
of Thailand

Th Ratchadamnoen Nok

Th Phra Sumen

Th Din So

⭐ 27

Th Nakhon Sawan

3

Th Ratchadamnoen Klang

4 Queen's
Gallery

Th Lan Luang

X 10

8 🟢 King Prajadhipok
Museum
🟢 Tha Phan
Fah

Th Din So

7 🟢
Wat
Ratchanatda

Th Mahachai

Th Boriphat

Golden
Mount &
Wat Saket

1 🟢

Khlong Saen Saeb

4

Bangkok
City Hall

Th Mahanop

X 13

Th Bamrung Meuang

Wat
uthat
2 🟢

Th Burapha
Th Siri Phong

X 11

Khlong Ong Ang

Th Bamrung Meuang

3 🟢 Soi Ban Baat

Ban Baat

Ⓝ 0 ———————— 500 m
0 ———————— 0.25 miles

5

Sights

Golden Mount & Wat Saket
BUDDHIST TEMPLE

1 Map p44, G4

A less conspicuous stop on the temple itinerary, the Golden Mount is an artificial hill from which Bangkok appears meditatively serene. Next door, Wat Saket has some interesting (and sometimes gory) Buddhist murals. Join the candlelit procession to the summit in November during the annual temple fair. (ภูเขาทอง & วัดสระเกศ; Th Boriphat; admission to summit of Golden Mount 10B; ⊙7.30am-5.30pm; 🚣klorng boat to Tha Phan Fah)

Wat Suthat
BUDDHIST TEMPLE

2 Map p44, E5

Other than being just plain huge and impressive, Wat Suthat also holds the highest royal temple grade. Inside the wí·hăhn (sanctuary for a Buddha sculpture) are intricate Jataka (stories of the Buddha) murals and Thailand's biggest surviving Sukhothai-era bronze Buddha. Over the road is the

Giant Swing (Sao Ching-Cha), site of a former Brahman festival in honour of Shiva. (วัดสุทัศน์; Th Bamrung Meuang; admission 20B; ⊙8.30am-8.30pm; 🚣klorng boat to Tha Phan Fah)

Ban Baat
NEIGHBOURHOOD

3 Map p44, F5

The only surviving village of three founded by Rama I. The residents of Ban Baat still hand-hammer eight pieces of steel (representing Buddha's eightfold path) into the distinctive alms bowls used by monks to receive morning food donations. Tourists – not temples – are the primary patrons these days and a bowl purchase is usually rewarded with a demonstration. (บ้านบาตร, Monk's Bowl Village; Soi Ban Baat; admission free; ⊙8am-5pm; 🚣klorng boat to Tha Phan Fah)

Queen's Gallery
ART GALLERY

4 Map p44, F3

This royal-funded museum presents five floors of rotating exhibitions of modern and traditionally influenced art. The building is sleek and contemporary and the artists hail from the upper echelons of the conservative Thai art world. The attached shop is filled with fine-arts books and gifts. (www.queengallery.org; 101 Th Ratchadamnoen Klang; admission 30B; ⊙10am-7pm Thu-Tue; 🚣klorng boat to Tha Phan Fah)

✓ Top Tip

Take the Boat

Boats – both the Chao Phraya River Express and the klorng boats – are a steady, if slow, way to reach Banglamphu, but remember that they only run until about 8pm on weekdays, 7pm on weekends.

Prayer bells, Wat Saket

Wat Bowonniwet
BUDDHIST TEMPLE

5 ⊚ Map p44, D2

Home to the Buddhist Mahamakut University, this royally affiliated monastery is the national headquarters of the Thammayut sect of Thai Buddhism. The murals in the *bòht* are noteworthy, and include Thai depictions of Western life during the early 19th century. The temple may be in ultra-casual Banglamphu, but it's also where the present king was ordained, so visitors must dress appropriately. (วัดบวรนิเวศวิหาร; www.watbowon.org; Th Phra Sumen; admission free; ⊗8.30am-5pm; ⚲Tha Phra Athit (Banglamphu))

Phra Sumen Fort & Santichaiprakan Park
FORT, PARK

6 ⊚ Map p44, C1

It's a tiny patch of greenery with a great river view and lots of evening action, including comical communal aerobics classes. The riverside pathway heading southwards makes for a serene promenade. The park's most prominent landmark is the blindingly white Phra Sumen Fort, which was built in 1783 to defend the city against a river invasion. (ป้อม พระสุเมรุ/สวนสันติชัยปราการ; Th Phra Athit; admission free; ⊗5am-10pm; ⚲Tha Phra Athit (Banglamphu))

Local Life
Pop & Lock

Most evenings the wide expanse in front of Bangkok's City Hall becomes a gathering place for young kids who meet to practice their breakdancing moves.

Wat Ratchanatda   BUDDHIST TEMPLE

7 ⊙ Map p44, F4

Built for Rama III (King Phranangklao; r 1824–51) in the 1840s, the design of this temple is said to derive from metal temples built in India and Sri Lanka more than 2000 years ago. At the back of the compound is a well-known market selling Buddhist *prá krêu·ang* (amulets) in all sizes, shapes and styles. (วัดราชนัดดาราม; cnr Th Ratchadamnoen Klang & Th Mahachai; admission free; ⊙8am–5pm; ☗klorng boat to Tha Phan Fah)

King Prajadhipok Museum   MUSEUM

8 ⊙ Map p44, G3

This collection uses modern techniques to relate the rather dramatic life of Rama VII (King Prajadhipok; r 1925–35). The museum occupies a grand neocolonial-style building constructed on the orders of Rama V for his favourite firm of Bond St merchants; it was the only foreign business allowed on the royal road linking Bangkok's two palace districts. (พิพิธภัณฑ์พระบาทสมเด็จพระปกเกล้าเจ้าอยู่หัว; 2 Th Lan Luang; admission 40B; ⊙9am–4pm Tue-Sun; ☗klorng boat to Tha Phan Fah)

October 14 Memorial   MONUMENT

9 ⊙ Map p44, D3

A peaceful amphitheatre commemorates the civilian demonstrators who were killed by the military during a pro-democracy rally on 14 October 1973. Over 200,000 people had assembled at the adjacent Democracy Monument to protest against the arrest of political campaigners and continuing military dictatorship. Although some in Thailand continue to deny it, photographs confirm that more than 70 demonstrators were killed. (อนุสรณ์สถาน ๑๔ ตุลา; cnr Th Ratchadamnoen Klang & Th Tanao; admission free; ⊙24hr; ☗klorng boat to Tha Phan Fah)

Eating

Krua Apsorn   THAI $$

10 ✖ Map p44, E3

This homey dining room is a favourite of members of the Thai royal family, and back in 2006 it was recognised as Bangkok's Best Restaurant by the *Bangkok Post*. Must-eat dishes include mussels fried with fresh herbs, the decadent crab fried in yellow chilli oil and the tortilla Española–like crab omelette. (www.kruaapsorn.com; Th Din So; mains 65-350B; ⊙10.30am-8pm Mon-Sat; ✱ 🖉; ☗klorng boat to Tha Phan Fah)

Jay Fai   THAI $$

11 ✖ Map p44, F4

You wouldn't think so by looking at her bare-bones dining room, but Jay Fai is known far and wide for serving

Understand

Th Khao San

Th Khao San, better known as Khao San Rd, is unlike anywhere else on earth. It's a clearing house of people either entering the liberated state of travelling in Southeast Asia or returning to the coddling bonds of first-world life, all coming together in a neon-lit melting pot in Banglamphu. Its uniqueness is best illustrated by a question: apart from airports, where else could you share space with the citizens of dozens of countries, people ranging from first-time backpackers scoffing banana pancakes to 75-year-old grandparents ordering G&Ts, and everyone in between?

The Emergence of an Icon

Th Khao San (*cow-sarn*), meaning 'uncooked rice', is perhaps the highest-profile bastard child of the age of independent travel. Of course, it hasn't always been this way. For its first two centuries it was just an unremarkable road in old Bangkok. The first guesthouses appeared in 1982, and as more backpackers arrived through the '80s, the old wooden homes were converted one by one into low-rent dosshouses. By the time Alex Garland's novel *The Beach* was published in 1997, with its opening scenes set on the seedier side of Khao San, staying here had become a rite of passage for backpackers coming to Southeast Asia.

The Khao San of Today

Publicity from Garland's book and the movie that followed pushed Khao San into the mainstream, romanticising the seedy, and stereotyping the backpackers it attracted as unwashed and counterculturalist. It also brought the long-simmering debate about the relative merits of Th Khao San to the top of backpacker conversations. Was it cool to stay on KSR? Was it uncool? Was this 'real travel' or just an international anywhere surviving on the few baht Western backpackers spent before they headed home to start high-earning careers? Was it really Thailand at all? Perceptions aside, today the strip continues to anticipate every traveller's need: meals to soothe homesickness, cafes and bars for swapping travel tales, tailors, travel agents, teeth whitening, secondhand books, hair braiding and, of course, the perennial Akha women trying to harass everyone they see into buying those croaking wooden frogs.

Bangkok's most expensive *pàt kêe mow* (drunkard's noodles – wide rice noodles fried with seafood and Thai herbs). Jay Fai doesn't have a roman-script sign, but is located directly across Th Mahachai from a 7-Eleven. (327 Th Mahachai; mains from 400B; ⏰3pm-2am Tue-Sun; 🔲; 🛥klorng boat to Tha Phan Fah)

Shoshana
ISRAELI $

12 🍴 Map p44, C2

One of Khao San's longest-running Israeli restaurants, Shoshana resembles your grandparents' living room, right down to the tacky wall art and plastic placemats. The 'I heart Shoshana' T-shirts worn by the wait staff may be a hopelessly optimistic description of employee morale, but the gut-filling chips-felafel-and-hummus plates leave nothing to be desired. (88 Th Chakraphong; mains 70-240B; ⏰10am-midnight; ❄🍴🔲; 🛥Tha Phra Athit (Banglamphu))

Thip Samai
THAI $

13 🍴 Map p44, F4

Brace yourself: you should be aware that the fried noodles sold from carts along Th Khao San have nothing to do with the dish known as *pàt tai*. Luckily, less than a five-minute túk-túk ride away is Thip Samai, home to the most legendary Thai-style fried noodles in town. Closed alternate Wednesdays. No roman-script sign. (www.thipsamai.com; 313 Th Mahachai; mains 25-120B; ⏰5.30pm-1.30am; 🔲; 🛥klorng boat to Tha Phan Fah)

Poj Spa Kar
THAI $

14 🍴 Map p44, D5

Pronounced *pôht sà·pah kahn*, this is allegedly the oldest restaurant in Bangkok, and it continues to maintain recipes handed down from a former palace cook. Be sure to order the simple but tasty lemon-grass omelette or the deliciously sour-sweet *gaang sôm*,

---

Local Life
Vegging Out in Banglamphu

Due to strong foreign influence, there's an abundance of vegetarian restaurants in the Banglamphu area. In addition to Hemlock (p51) and Shoshana (p50), both of which have big meat-free sections, alternatives include the following:

▶ **Arawy Vegetarian Food** (Map p44, E4; 152 Th Din So; mains 20-40B; ⏰7am-8pm; 🍴🔲; 🛥klorng boat to Tha Phan Fah) Prepared meat-free curries, dips and stir-fries.

▶ **Ranee Guesthouse** (Map p44, C2; 77 Trok Mayom; mains 70-320B; ⏰8am-10pm; 🍴🔲; 🛥Tha Phra Athit (Banglamphu)) Guesthouse-bound restaurant with big veg menu.

▶ **May Kaidee's** (Map p44, D1; www.maykaidee.com; 33 Th Samsen; mains 50-100B; ⏰9am-10pm; ❄🍴🔲; 🛥Tha Phra Athit (Banglamphu)) A longstanding restaurant that also houses a veggie Thai cooking school.

a traditional central Thai soup. No roman-script sign. (443 Th Tanao; mains 65-200B; ⏱12.30-8.30pm; ❄💳; 🚤klorng boat to Tha Phan Fah)

Roti-Mataba   MUSLIM-THAI $

15 🍴 Map p44, C1

This classic Bangkok eatery may have become a bit too big for its britches in recent years, but it still serves tasty Thai-Muslim dishes such as roti, *gaang mát·sà·màn* (Muslim curry), a brilliantly sour fish curry, and *má·tà·bà* (a sort of stuffed Muslim-style pancake). An upstairs air-con dining area and outdoor tables provide additional seating for its loyal fans. (136 Th Phra Athit; mains 50-90B; ⏱9am-10pm Tue-Sun; ❄🌿💳; 🚤Tha Phra Athit (Banglamphu))

Chote Chitr   THAI $

16 🍴 Map p44, D5

This third-generation shophouse restaurant boasting just six tables is a Bangkok foodie landmark. The kitchen can be inconsistent and the service consistently grumpy, but when they're on, dishes like *mèe gròrp* (crispy fried noodles) and *yam tòoa ploo* (wing-bean salad) are in a class of their own. (146 Th Phraeng Phuthon; mains 30-200B; ⏱11am-10pm; 💳; 🚤klorng boat to Tha Phan Fah)

Hemlock   THAI $

17 🍴 Map p44, B2

Taking full advantage of its cosy shophouse location, this perennial favourite has enough style to feel like a special

Street market, Banglamphu

AUSTIN BUSH/GETTY IMAGES ©

night out but doesn't skimp on flavour or preparation. The eclectic menu reads like an ancient literary work, reviving old dishes from aristocratic kitchens across the country. (56 Th Phra Athit; mains 60-220B; ⏱4pm-midnight; ❄🌿💳; 🚤Tha Phra Athit (Banglamphu))

Isan Restaurants   NORTHEASTERN THAI $

18 🍴 Map p44, G2

When a boxing match is on at Ratchadamnoen Stadium, these places are busy serving plates of Isan (northeastern) staples like *gài yâhng* (grilled chicken), *sôm·đam* (green papaya salad) and *kôw nĭaw* (sticky rice). (off Th Ratchadamnoen Nok; mains 30-120B; ⏱10am-10pm; ❄; 🚤klorng boat to Tha Phan Fah)

Top Tip

What's Your Name?

Banglamphu means 'Place of Lamphu', a reference to the *lam·poo* tree (*Duabanga grandiflora*) that was once prevalent in the area.

Kimleng   THAI $

19 Map p44, D3

This tiny family-run restaurant specialises in the dishes and flavours of central Thailand. It's a good place to whet your appetite with an authentic *yam* (Thai-style salad) such as *yam ʰblah dùk foo*, a mixture of crispy catfish and mango. (158-160 Th Tanao; mains 20-60B; ⏰10am-10pm Mon-Sat; ✱ⓜ; ⛴klorng boat to Tha Phan Fah)

Ann's Sweet   CAFE $

20 Map p44, C1

Anshada, a native of Bangkok, is a graduate of the Cordon Bleu cooking program. Come to her cozy cafe for coffee and some of the most authentic Western-style desserts you'll find anywhere in Bangkok. (138 Th Phra Athit; mains 75-150B; ⏰10am-10pm; ✱ⓜ; ⛴Tha Phra Athit (Banglamphu))

Drinking

Hippie de Bar   BAR

21 Map p44, C2

Our vote for Banglamphu's best bar, Hippie boasts a funky retro vibe and indoor and outdoor seating, all set to a sophisticated indie/pop soundtrack that you're unlikely to hear elsewhere in town. Despite being located smack-dab in the middle of Th Khao San, there are surprisingly few foreign faces, and it's a great place to make some new Thai friends. (46 Th Khao San; ⏰6pm-2am; ⛴Tha Phra Athit (Banglamphu))

Phra Nakorn Bar & Gallery   BAR

22 Map p44, D3

Located an ambivalent arm's length from the hype of Th Khao San, Phra Nakorn Bar is a home away from hovel for students and arty types, with eclectic decor and changing gallery exhibits. Our tip: head directly for the breezy rooftop and order some of the bar's cheap 'n' tasty Thai food. (58/2 Soi Damnoen Klang Tai; ⏰5pm-1am; ⛴klorng boat to Tha Phan Fah)

Taksura   BAR

23 Map p44, D3

There's scant English-language signage to lead you to this 90-year-old mansion in the heart of old Bangkok, which is all the better, according to the overwhelmingly Thai, uni/artsy crowd that frequents the place. Take a seat outside to soak up the breezes and go domestic by ordering some spicy nibbles with your drinks. (156/1 Th Tanao; ⏰5pm-1am; ⛴klorng boat to Tha Phan Fah)

Rolling Bar   BAR

24 🚇 Map p44, E2

An escape from hectic Th Khao San
is a good-enough excuse to schlep
to this quiet canalside boozer. Live
music and capable bar snacks are
good reasons to stay. (Th Prachathipatai;
⏱5pm-midnight; 🚤klorng boat to Tha
Phan Fah)

Entertainment

Brick Bar   LIVE MUSIC

25 ⭐ Map p44, D3

This basement pub, one of our fave
destinations in Bangkok for live music, hosts a nightly revolving cast of
Thai bands for an almost 100% Thai
crowd – many of whom will end the
night dancing on the tables. Brick Bar
can get infamously packed, so be sure
to get there early if you want a table.
(basement, Buddy Lodge, 265 Th Khao San;
admission 100B; ⏱8pm-1am; 🚤Tha Phra
Athit (Banglamphu))

Ratchadamnoen Stadium   THAI BOXING

26 ⭐ Map p44, G2

Ratchadamnoen Stadium, Bangkok's
oldest and most venerable venue
for *moo·ay tai* (Thai boxing, also
spelt *muay thai*) hosts matches on
Monday, Wednesday, Thursday and
Sunday starting at 6.30pm. Be sure
to buy tickets from the official ticket
counter, not from the touts who hang
around outside the entrance. (off Th
Ratchadamnoen Nok; tickets 3rd/2nd class/
ringside 1000/1500/2000B; 🚤klorng boat to
Tha Phan Fah)

Brown Sugar   LIVE MUSIC

27 ⭐ Map p44, F3

This longstanding live music den has
found a new home in Old Bangkok. It
touts itself as a 'jazz boutique', but the
tunes range from vocal jazz to perky
pop. Other reasons to stop by include
the cosy atmosphere and the deep-
fried pork knuckle, not the overpriced
drinks. (www.brownsugarbangkok.com; 469

Local Life
Buy-a-Buddha

The stretch of Th Bamrung Meuang (one of Bangkok's oldest streets and
originally an elephant path leading to the Grand Palace) from Th Mahachai
to Th Tanao is lined with shops selling all manner of Buddhist religious
paraphernalia. Behind the storefronts, back-room workshops produce
gigantic bronze Buddha images for *wát* all over Thailand. You probably don't
need a Buddha statue or an eerily lifelike model of a famous monk, but
looking is fun, and who knows when you might need to do a great deal of
merit making.

Understand
Thai Boxing

More formally known as Phahuyut (from the Pali-Sanskrit *bhahu* or 'arm' and *yodha* or 'combat'), Thailand's ancient martial art of *moo·ay tai* (Thai boxing; also spelt *muay thai*) is one of the kingdom's most striking national icons.

An Ancient Tradition
Many martial-arts aficionados agree that *moo·ay tai* is the most efficient, effective and generally unbeatable form of ring-centred, hand-to-hand combat practised today. After the Siamese were defeated at Ayuthaya in 1767, several expert *moo·ay boh·rahn* (from which contemporary *moo·ay tai* is derived) fighters were among the prisoners hauled off to Burma. A few years later a festival was held; one of the Thai fighters, Nai Khanom Tom, was ordered to take on prominent Burmese boxers for the entertainment of the king and to determine which martial art was most effective. He promptly dispatched nine opponents in a row and, as legend has it, was offered money or beautiful women as a reward; he promptly took two new wives.

The Modern Game
In the early days of the sport, combatants' fists were wrapped in thick horsehide for maximum impact with minimum knuckle damage; tree bark and seashells were used to protect the groin from lethal kicks. But the high incidence of death and physical injury led the Thai government to ban *moo·ay tai* in the 1920s; in the 1930s the sport was revived under a modern set of regulations. Bouts were limited to five three-minute rounds separated by two-minute breaks. Contestants had to wear international-style gloves and trunks and their feet were taped – to this day no shoes are worn. In spite of all these concessions to safety, today all surfaces of the body remain fair targets and any part of the body except the head may be used to strike an opponent. Common blows include high kicks to the neck, elbow thrusts to the face and head, knee hooks to the ribs and low kicks to the calf. Punching is considered the weakest of all blows, and kicking merely a way to 'soften up' one's opponent; knee and elbow strikes are decisive in most matches.

Th Phra Sumen; ⏰5pm-1am Mon-Thu, to 2am
Sat & Sun; 🚤Tha Phra Athit (Banglamphu))

Ad Here the 13th
LIVE MUSIC

28 ⭐ Map p44, D1

Located beside Khlong Ong Ang, Ad
Here is everything a neighbourhood
joint should be: lots of regulars, cold
beer and heart-warming tunes deliv-
ered by a masterful house band starting at 10pm. Everyone knows each
other, so don't be shy about mingling.
(13 Th Samsen; ⏰6pm-midnight; 🚤Tha Phra
Athit (Banglamphu))

Shopping

Th Khao San Market
MARKET

29 🔒 Map p44, C2

The main guesthouse strip in
Banglamphu is a day-and-night shopping bazaar, selling all but the baby
and the bathwater. Cheap T-shirts,
trendy purses, wooden frogs, fuzzy
puppets, bootleg CDs, hemp clothing, fake student ID cards, knock-off
designer wear, souvenirs, corn on
the cob, orange juice... You name it,
they've got it here. (Th Khao San; ⏰10am-
midnight; 🚤Tha Phra Athit (Banglamphu))

Nittaya Curry Shop
FOOD & DRINK

30 🔒 Map p44, C2

Follow your nose: Nittaya is famous
throughout Thailand for her pungent

🔍 Local Life
Off the Beaten Track
Although Th Khao San remains
associated with foreign tourists,
in recent years it's also become
a popular nightlife destination for
young locals. For an almost entirely
local drinking scene, check out the
live-music pubs along Th Phra Athit
or the low-key bars south of Th
Ratchadamnoen Klang.

but high-quality curry pastes. Pick
up a couple of takeaway canisters for
prospective dinner parties or peruse
the snack and gift sections, where
visitors to Bangkok load up on local
specialities for friends back in the
provinces. No roman-script sign. (136-
40 Th Chakhraphong; ⏰9am-7pm Mon-Sat;
🚤Tha Phra Athit (Banglamphu))

Taekee Taekon
HANDICRAFTS

31 🔒 Map p44, C1

This atmospheric shop has a decent
selection of Thai textiles from the
country's main silk-producing areas,
especially northern Thailand, as well
as the type of assorted local knick-
knackery and interesting postcards
not widely available elsewhere. (118 Th
Phra Athit; ⏰9am-6pm Mon-Sat; 🚤Tha Phra
Athit (Banglamphu))

Top Sights
Dusit Palace Park

Getting There

S Phaya Thai exit 2 and taxi

⚓ Tha Thewet

Following the first European tour of Rama V (King Chulalongkorn; r 1868–1910) in 1897, he returned home with visions of European castles and set about transforming those styles into a uniquely Thai expression, today's Dusit Palace Park. The royal palace, throne hall and minor palaces for extended family were all moved here, and were supplemented with beaux arts institutions and Victorian manor houses. The resulting fascinating architectural mishmash and the expansive gardens make the compound a worthwhile escape from the chaos of modern Bangkok.

Abhisek Dusit Throne Hall

Don't Miss

Vimanmek Teak Mansion

Originally constructed on Ko Si Chang in 1868 and moved to the present site in 1910, Vimanmek Teak Mansion contains 81 rooms, halls and anterooms, and is said to be the world's largest golden-teak building, allegedly built without the use of a single nail. Compulsory tours (in English) leave every half-hour between 9.45am and 3.15pm, and last about an hour.

Abhisek Dusit Throne Hall

Moorish palaces and Victorian mansions are the main influences on this intricate building of porticoes and fretwork fused with a distinctive Thai character. Today, the hall displays regional handiwork crafted by members of the Promotion of Supplementary Occupations & Related Techniques (Support), a charity foundation sponsored by Queen Sirikit.

Royal Elephant Museum

Near the Th U Thong Nai entrance are two stables that once housed three white elephants – animals whose albinism automatically make them crown property. One of the structures contains artefacts outlining the importance of elephants in Thai history and explaining their various rankings according to physical characteristics. The second stable holds a sculptural representation of a living royal white elephant.

Other Exhibits

Near the Th Ratchawithi entrance, two residence halls display the **HM King Bhumibol Photography Exhibitions**, a collection of photographs and paintings by the present monarch. The **Ancient Cloth Museum** presents a beautiful collection of traditional silks and cottons.

วังสวนดุสิต

bounded by Th Ratchawithi, Th U-Thong Nai & Th Ratchasima

adult/child 100/50B

🕙9.30am-3.15pm Tue-Sun

🚢Tha Thewet, **S**Phaya Thai exit 2 & taxi

☑ Top Tips

▶ Entry is free if you're holding a same-day ticket from Wat Phra Kaew & Grand Palace (p24).

▶ Visitors should wear long pants (no capri pants) or long skirts and sleeved shirts.

✗ Take a Break

For a cheap and cheerful riverside lunch, try **Kaloang Home Kitchen** (Th Si Ayuthaya; mains 60-170B; 🕙11am-11pm; 🚢Tha Thewet). Or make the short walk to a branch of the award-winning Thai restaurant **Krua Apsorn** (www.kruaapsorn.com; 503-505 Th Samsen; mains 40-250B; 🕙10.30am-7.30pm Mon-Fri, to 6pm Sat; ❄; 🚢Tha Thewet).

Explore

Chinatown

Although many generations removed from the mainland, Bangkok's Chinatown could be a bosom brother of any Chinese city. The streets are crammed with shark-fin restaurants, gaudy yellow-gold and jade shops, and flashing neon signs with Chinese characters. It's Bangkok's most hectic neighbourhood and, as such, is a great place in which to get lost.

The Sights in a Day

Start your day early by beating the tour buses to the immense golden Buddha at **Wat Traimit** (p60). Continue, crossing through the frenetic market alleyway that is **Talat Mai** (p65), to the maze-like Chinese-style temple, **Wat Mangkon Kamalawat** (p65).

Make your way by foot or taxi to **Phahurat** (p66), Bangkok's Little India. Take lunch at **Royal India** (p70) and, if you've got the space, a post-lunch dessert at **Old Siam Plaza** (p70).

Chinatown begins to pick up again in the early evening, and this is the best time to return to the area and follow our food-based **tour** (p62) of the neighbourhood. After dinner, bide your time with a cocktail and live jazz at **Cotton** (p71). When it's as late as you're willing to stay up, cross over to the nocturnal flower market at **Pak Khlong Talat** (p65).

◉ Top Sights
Wat Traimit (p60)

○ Local Life
A Taste of Chinatown (p62)

♥ Best of Bangkok

Temples
Wat Traimit (p60)

Wat Mangkon Kamalawat (p65)

Street Food
Nai Mong Hoi Thod (p62)

Th Phadungdao Seafood Stalls (p63)

Markets
Pak Khlong Talat (p65)

Talat Mai (p65)

Museums
Yaowarat Chinatown Heritage Center (p61)

Live Music
Cotton (p71)

Getting There

Ⓜ Hua Lamphong

⚓ **River ferry** Tha Marine Department, Tha Ratchawong and Tha Saphan Phut (Memorial Bridge)

Top Sights
Wat Traimit (Golden Buddha)

Wat Traimit, also known as the Temple of the Golden Buddha, is home to the world's largest gold statue, a gleaming, 3m-tall, 5.5-tonne Buddha image with a mysterious past and a current value of more than US$250 million. Sculpted in the graceful Sukhothai style, the image is thought to date from as long ago as the 13th century, but if it is possible for a Buddha image to lead a double life, then this piece has most certainly done so.

วัด ไตรมิตร, Temple of the Golden Buddha

Map p64, D3

Th Mitthaphap (Th Traimit)

admission 40B

8am-5pm Tue-Sun

Tha Ratchawong,
Hua Lamphong exit 1

Golden Buddha

Don't Miss

Golden Buddha

The star attraction at Wat Traimit is the gold Buddha image. Located on the 4th floor of Phra Maha Mondop, the temple compound's imposing marble structure, the image was originally 'discovered' some 60 years ago beneath a stucco or plaster exterior when it fell from a crane while being moved. It's thought that the covering was added to protect the statue from marauding hordes.

Yaowarat Chinatown Heritage Center

On the 2nd floor of Phra Maha Mondop is this relatively small but engaging **museum** (admission 100B; ◷8am-5pm Tue-Sun), which houses multimedia exhibits on Chinese immigration to Thailand, as well as on the history of Bangkok's Chinatown and its residents. Particularly fun are the miniature dioramas that depict important cultural facets of Thai-Chinese life.

Phra Buddha Maha Suwanna Patimakorn Exhibition

On the 3rd floor of the marble structure, this museumlike **exhibition** (admission 100B; ◷8am-5pm Tue-Sun) recounts how Wat Traimit's Buddha statue was made, discovered and transported to its current home. If you've ever wondered how to make – or move – a 5.5-tonne gold Buddha statue, your questions will be answered here.

Phra Maha Mondop

In 2009 a new home for the statue was built. Combining marble, Chinese-style balustrades and a steep Thai-style roof, it's one of the taller buildings in Chinatown, and the golden spire can be seen from blocks away. Surrounding it is a narrow strip of grass watered via mist fountains, and the usual Thai temple buildings.

☑ Top Tips

▸ Wat Traimit is a short walk from the MRT stop at Hua Lamphong.

▸ Wat Traimit is not open to the public on Mondays.

▸ Don't overlook the two interesting museums located in the same structure as the Golden Buddha.

✕ Take a Break

Chinese food rules in this part of town, but if noodles aren't your thing, head over to Phahurat, Bangkok's Little India, where you can have a South Asian–style meal at Royal India (p70). Alternatively, consider making a sweet diversion from Wat Traimit at Old Siam Plaza (p70), a vast food hall where every type of Thai sweet is made right before your eyes.

Local Life
A Taste of Chinatown

Street food rules in Chinatown, making the area ideal for a culinary adventure. Although many vendors stay open late, the more popular stalls tend to sell out quickly, and the best time to feast in this area is from 7pm to 9pm. Don't attempt this walk on a Monday, when most of the city's street vendors stay at home. Many of the stalls don't have roman-script signs.

1 Nai Mong Hoi Thod

Start at the intersection of Th Plaeng Nam and Th Charoen Krung. Head north along Th Phlap Phla Chai until you reach **Nai Mong Hoi Thod** (นาย หมง; 539 Th Phlap Phla Chai; ⏰5-10pm Tue-Sun; 🚤Tha Ratchawong, Ⓜ️Hua Lamphong exit 1 & taxi), renowned for its delicious *or sòo·an* (mussels or oysters fried with egg and a sticky batter).

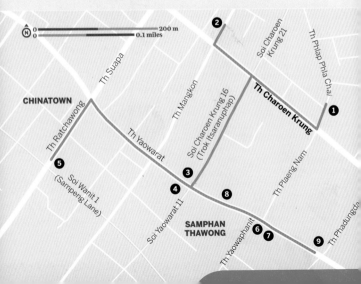

❷ Jék Pûi

Backtrack to Th Charoen Krung and turn right. Upon reaching Th Mangkon make a right. To your left is **Jék Pûi** (เจ็กปุ้ย; Th Mangkon; ⏱4-8pm Tue-Sun; ⛴Tha Ratchawong, Ⓜ Hua Lamphong exit 1 & taxi), a table-less stall renowned for its mild Chinese-style Thai curries.

❸ Gŏo·ay đĕe·o kôo·a gài

Cross Th Charoen Krung again, turn left, and head east to Soi 16 (aka Trok Itsaranuphap). At the end of this lane you'll see a gentleman making **gŏo·ay đĕe·o kôo·a gài** (Soi 6, Th Yaowarat; ⏱5-10pm Tue-Sun; ⛴Tha Ratchawong, Ⓜ Hua Lamphong exit 1 & taxi), wide rice noodles fried with chicken, egg and garlic oil.

❹ Nay Lék Ûan

Upon emerging at Th Yaowarat, cross over to the busy market area directly across the street. The first vendor on the right, **Nay Lék Ûan** (นายเล็กอ้วน; Soi Yaowarat 11; ⏱5pm-midnight; ⛴Tha Ratchawong, Ⓜ Hua Lamphong exit 1 & taxi), sells *gŏo·ay jáp nám săi*, an intensely peppery broth containing carpet-roll-like rice noodles and pork offal.

❺ Phat Thai Ratchawong

Go west on Th Yaowarat. Turn left onto Th Ratchawong, where **Phat Thai Ratchawong** (Th Ratchawong; ⏱7-11pm Tue-Sun; ⛴Tha Ratchawong, Ⓜ Hua Lamphong exit 1 & taxi), a stall run by a Chinese-Thai couple, offers a unique version of *pàt tai* – Thailand's most famous dish – fried over coals and served in banana leaf cups.

❻ Mangkorn Khŏw

Backtrack along Th Yaowarat to the corner of Th Yaowaphanit, where you'll see **Mangkorn Khŏw** (cnr Th Yaowarat & Th Yaowaphanit; ⏱5-11pm Tue-Sun; ⛴Tha Ratchawong, Ⓜ Hua Lamphong exit 1 & taxi), a street stall selling tasty *bà·mèe*, Chinese-style wheat noodles served with crab or barbecued pork.

❼ Boo·a loy nám kĭng

Adjacent to Mangkorn Khŏw is a no-name **stall** (cnr Th Yaowarat & Th Yaowaphanit; ⏱5-11pm Tue-Sun; ✍; Ⓜ Hua Lamphong exit 1 & taxi, Tha Ratchawong) that does Chinese-Thai desserts, including delicious *boo·a loy nám kĭng*, dumplings stuffed with rich black sesame paste and served in a spicy ginger broth.

❽ Hua Seng Hong

Cross to the north side of Th Yaowarat. On your left you'll see **Hua Seng Hong** (371-373 Th Yaowarat; mains 100-1050B; ⏱9am-1am; ❄; ⛴Tha Ratchawong, Ⓜ Hua Lamphong exit 1 & taxi), a modern Chinese place that's one of the relatively few air-conditioned restaurants in the area.

❾ Th Phadungdao Seafood Stalls

Continue east until you reach the intersection with Th Phadungdao; this corner is the unmistakable location of **Lek & Rut and TK** (cnr Th Phadungdao & Th Yaowarat; mains 180-300B; ⏱4pm-midnight Tue-Sun; Ⓜ Hua Lamphong exit 1 & taxi, Tha Ratchawong), two extremely popular and nearly identical open-air seafood joints.

E

Th Luang

Khlong Ong Ang

Th Krung Kasem

Th Mittaphan

Hualamphong
Train Station

Th Phra
Ram IV

Hua Lamphong

Th Mitthaphap
(Th Traimit)

Th Charoen Krung

Holy
Rosary
Church 12

Flashlight
Market 4

Th Maitrichit

Th Phlap
Phla Chai

Th Mangkon

Wat Mangkon Kamalawat 3

Wong
Wian 22
Karakada

Th
Santiphap

Phadungdao

Th Songsawat

Wat Traimit

Soi Charoen Phanit

Talat
Noi 6

Soi Phanurangsi

Tha Marine
Department

D

Th Suapa

Th Charoen
Krung

Soi Charoen Krung 16
(Trok Itsaranuphap)

Talat 2
Mai

Th Chiangmai

Th Songwat

C

Th Yaowarat

Sampeng
Lane 8

Soi Wanit 1 (Sampeng Lane)

CHINATOWN

Th
Ratchawong

Tha
Ratchawong

Mae Nam Chao Phraya

Th Mahachai

Khlong Ong Ang

Th Burapha

Gurdwara
Siri Guru Singh
Sabha

Phahurat 5

11

14

7

Th Chakrawat

Saphan
Phut Night
Bazaar 10

400 m
0.2 miles

Th Somdet Chao Phraya

B

15

13

Th Charoen Krung

Th Triphet

Th Ban Mo

Th Chakraphet

Pak Khlong
Talat 1

Saphan Phut (Memorial)
Bridge

Phra
Pokklao
Bridge

Church of
Santa Cruz

Th Prachathipok

A

Sarantom
Royal
Garden

Th Phahurat

1

2

3

9

4

For reviews see	
◆ Top Sights	p60
⊙ Sights	p65
✕ Eating	p70
⊕ Entertainment	p71

Sights

Pak Khlong Talat   MARKET

1 Map p64, A2

This wholesale flower market has become a tourist attraction in its own right. Come late at night when the endless piles of delicate orchids, rows of roses and stacks of button carnations are a sight to be seen, and the shirtless porters wheeling blazing piles of colour set the place in motion. (ปากคลองตลาด, Flower Market; Th Chakraphet; ⊙24hr; 🚤Tha Saphan Phut (Memorial Bridge))

Talat Mai   MARKET

2 Map p64, C2

Nudge your way deep into one of Chinatown's famous capillaries, where vendors sell dried goods, half-alive filleted fish and vats of unidentifiable pickled things. The soi's poetic finale (north of Th Charoen Krung) is lined with stalls selling elaborate funeral offerings and 'passports to heaven' that include paper iPhones and cars to accompany loved ones into the next life. (ตลาดใหม่; Soi Charoen Krung 16 (Trok Itsaranuphap)/Soi 6, Th Yaowarat; ⊙6am-7pm; 🚤Tha Ratchawong, Ⓜ Hua Lamphong exit 1 & taxi)

Wat Mangkon
Kamalawat   CHINESE TEMPLE

3 Map p64, D2

Explore the cryptlike sermon halls of this busy Chinese temple to find Bud-

✓ Top Tip

Day Off

Most of Bangkok's street-food vendors close up shop on Monday, so don't plan on eating in Chinatown – where most of the food is street-based – on this day.

dhist, Taoist and Confucian shrines. During the annual Vegetarian Festival, religious and culinary activities are centred here. But almost any time of day or night this temple is busy with worshippers lighting incense, filling the ever-burning altar lamps with oil and making offerings to their ancestors. (วัดมังกรกมลาวาส, Leng Noi Yee; Th Charoen Krung; admission free; ⊙6am-6pm; 🚤Tha Ratchawong, Ⓜ Hua Lamphong exit 1 & taxi)

Flashlight Market   MARKET

4 Map p64, D1

This street market extends west from the Phlap Phla Chai intersection, forging a trail of antiques, secondhand items and, well, sometimes just plain junk, along the area's footpaths. It's open for 24 hours on the weekend, but is at its busiest on Saturday night, when a flashlight is needed to see many of the goods for sale. (ตลาดไฟฉาย; cnr Th Phlap Phla Chai & Th Luang; ⊙5pm Sat-5pm Sun; 🚤Tha Ratchawong, Ⓜ Hua Lamphong exit 1 & taxi)

IGOR PRAHIN/GETTY IMAGES ©

Church of Santa Cruz (p69)

Phahurat

NEIGHBOURHOOD

5 ⊙ Map p64, B2

Heaps of South Asian traders set up shop in this small but bustling Little India, where everything from Bollywood movies to bindis is sold by small-time traders. Much of the emphasis is on cloth, and Phahurat proffers boisterous Bollywood-coloured textiles, traditional Thai dance costumes, tiaras, sequins, wigs and other accessories. Phahurat is located west and east of Th Chakrawat, extending roughly between Th Yaowarat and Tha Saphan Phut (Memorial Bridge). (พาหุรัด; ⊙9am-5pm; ☸Tha Saphan Phut (Memorial Bridge))

Talat Noi

NEIGHBOURHOOD

6 ⊙ Map p64, D4

This microcosm of soi life is named after a small (nóy) market that sets up between Soi 22 and Soi 20, off Th Charoen Krung. Wandering here you'll find streamlike soi turning in on themselves, weaving through people's living rooms, noodle shops and grease-stained machine shops; it's also one of the best places to come during the yearly Vegetarian Festival. (ตลาดน้อย; ⊙7am-7pm; ☸Tha Marine Department)

Hualamphong Train Station

HISTORICAL BUILDING

7 ⊙ Map p64, E3

At the southeastern edge of Chinatown, Hualamphong Train Station, Bangkok's main train terminal, was built by Dutch architects and engineers between 1910 and 1916. If you can zone out of the chaos for a moment, look for the vaulted iron roof and neoclassical portico that were a state-of-the-art engineering feat. (สถานีรถไฟหัวลำโพง; off Th Phra Ram IV; Ⓜ Hua Lamphong exit 2)

Sampeng Lane

MARKET

8 ⊙ Map p64, C2

Sampeng Lane (officially known as Soi Wanit 1) is a narrow artery that runs parallel to Th Yaowarat and bisects the commercial areas of Chinatown and Phahurat. The area is lined with wholesale shops of 'Made in China' hair accessories, pens, stickers, household wares and beeping, flashing

Understand

The Chinese Influence

In many ways Bangkok is a Chinese, as much as a Thai, city. The Chinese presence in Bangkok predates the founding of the city, when Thonburi Si Mahasamut was little more than a Chinese trading outpost on Mae Nam Chao Phraya. In the 1780s, during the construction of the new capital under Rama I (King Phraphutthayotfa; r 1782–1809), Hokkien, Teochew and Hakka Chinese were hired as labourers. Eventually these labourers and entrepreneurs were relocated to the districts of Yaowarat and Sampeng, today known as Bangkok's Chinatown.

Roots in Business
During the reign of Rama I, many Chinese began to move up in status and wealth. They controlled many of Bangkok's shops and businesses, and because of increased trading ties with China, were responsible for an immense expansion in Thailand's market economy. Visiting Europeans during the 1820s were astonished by the number of Chinese trading ships on Mae Nam Chao Phraya, and some assumed that the Chinese formed the majority of Bangkok's population.

An Emerging Aristocracy
The newfound wealth of certain Chinese trading families created one of Thailand's first elite classes that was not directly related to royalty. Known as jôw sŏo·a, these 'merchant lords' eventually obtained additional status by accepting official posts and royal titles, as well as offering their daughters to the royal family. At one point, Rama V (King Chulalongkorn; r 1868–1910) took a Chinese consort. Today it is believed that more than half of the people in Bangkok can claim some Chinese ancestry.

Cultural Integration
During the reign of Rama III (King Phranangklao; r 1824–51), the Thai capital began to absorb many elements of Chinese food, design, fashion and literature. By the beginning of the 20th century, the ubiquity of Chinese culture, coupled with the tendency of the Chinese men to marry Thai women and assimilate into Thai culture, had resulted in relatively little difference between the Chinese and their Siamese counterparts.

Understand

The King

- -

If you see a yellow Rolls-Royce flashing by along Bangkok avenues, accompanied by a police escort, you've probably just caught a glimpse of Thailand's longest-reigning monarch – and the longest-reigning living monarch in the world – King Bhumibol Adulyadej.

The Man on the Throne
Also known in English as Rama IX, Bhumibol Adulyadej was born in 1927 in the USA, where his father, Prince Mahidol, was studying medicine at Harvard. Fluent in English, French, German and Thai, Bhumibol ascended the throne in 1946 following the death of his brother Rama VIII (King Ananda Mahidol; r 1935–46), who reigned for just over 11 years before dying under mysterious circumstances. An ardent jazz composer and saxophonist when he was younger, Rama IX has hosted jam sessions with the likes of jazz greats Woody Herman and Benny Goodman. His compositions are often played on Thai radio. The king is also recognised for his extensive development projects, particularly in rural areas of Thailand. Rama IX and Queen Sirikit have four children: Princess Ubol Ratana (b 1951), Crown Prince Maha Vajiralongkorn (b 1952), Princess Mahachakri Sirindhorn (b 1955) and Princess Chulabhorn (b 1957).

The Twilight of an Era
After more than 60 years in power, and having recently reached his 85th birthday, Rama IX is preparing for his succession. For the last few years the Crown Prince has performed most of the royal ceremonies the king would normally perform, such as presiding over the Royal Ploughing Ceremony, changing the attire on the Emerald Buddha and handing out academic degrees at university commencements.

Royal Etiquette
Along with nation and religion, the monarchy is highly regarded in Thai society, and negative comment about Rama IX or any member of the royal family is a social as well as a legal taboo. For an objective English-language biography of the king's life and accomplishments, *King Bhumibol Adulyadej: A Life's Work* (Editions Didier Millet, 2010) is available in many Bangkok bookshops.

knick-knacks. (สำเพ็ง; Soi Wanit 1; ⊘8am-6pm; 🚤Tha Ratchawong, MHua Lamphong exit 1 & taxi)

Church of Santa Cruz CHURCH

9 ◎ Map p64, A3

Centuries before Sukhumvit became Bangkok's international district, the Portuguese claimed *fa·ràng* (Western) supremacy and built the Church of Santa Cruz in the 1700s. The surviving church dates to 1913. Small village streets break off from the main courtyard into the area; on Soi Kuti Jiin 3, several houses sell Portuguese-inspired cakes and sweets. (โบสถ์ซางตาครู้ส; Soi Kuti Jiin; admission free; ⊘7am-noon Sat & Sun; 🚤Tha Pak Talat (Atsadang))

Saphan Phut Night Bazaar MARKET

10 ◎ Map p64, B3

On the Bangkok side of Saphan Phut (Memorial Bridge), this low-key night market has bucketloads of cheap clothes, late-night snacking and a lot of people-watching. (ตลาดนัดสะพานพุทธ; Th Saphan Phut; ⊘8pm-midnight Tue-Sun; 🚤Tha Saphan Phut (Memorial Bridge))

Gurdwara Siri Guru Singh Sabha SIKH TEMPLE

11 ◎ Map p64, B2

Just off Th Chakrawat is this gold-domed Sikh temple – allegedly one of the largest outside India. Prasada

(blessed food offered to Hindu or Sikh temple attendees) is distributed among devotees every morning around 9am, and if you arrive on a Sikh festival day, you can partake in the *langar* (communal Sikh meal) served in the temple. (พระศาสนสถานคุรุดวารา; off Th Chakrawat; ⊘9am-5pm; 🚤Tha Saphan Phut (Memorial Bridge))

Holy Rosary Church CHURCH

12 ◎ Map p64, D4

When a Portuguese contingent moved across the river to the present-day Talat Noi area of Chinatown in 1787, they were given this piece of land and they built the Holy Rosary Church, known in Thai as Wat Kalawan, from the Portuguese 'Calvario'. The current structure dates back to 1898. (วัดแม่พระลูกประคำกาลหว่าร์; Th Yotha; admission free; ⊘Mass 7.30pm Mon-Sat, 8am, 10am & 7.30pm Sun; 🚤Tha Marine Department)

Local Life
Waving the Yellow Flag

During the annual Vegetarian Festival in September/October, Bangkok's Chinatown becomes a virtual orgy of nonmeat cuisine. The festivities centre on Chinatown's main street, Th Yaowarat, and the Talat Noi area, but food shops and stalls all over the city post yellow flags to announce their meat-free status.

Eating

Old Siam Plaza
THAI SWEETS $

13 🍴 Map p64, B1

Sugar junkies, be sure to include this stop on your Bangkok eating itinerary. The ground floor of this shopping centre is a candy land of traditional Thai sweets and snacks, most made right before your eyes. (cnr Th Phahurat & Th Triphet; mains 30-90B; ⊙6am-7pm; 🌂; 🚢Tha Saphan Phut (Memorial Bridge))

Royal India
INDIAN $

14 🍴 Map p64, B2

A windowless dining room of 10 tables in a dark alley may not be everybody's ideal lunch destination, but this legendary north Indian place continues to draw foodies despite the lack of aesthetics. Try any of the delicious breads or rich curries, and finish with a homemade Punjabi sweet. (392/1 Th Chakraphet; mains 70-195B; ⊙10am-10pm; 🌂 🖉 📖; 🚢Tha Saphan Phut (Memorial Bridge))

Understand
Chinatown's Shopping Streets

Chinatown is the neighbourhood version of a big-box store divided up into categories of consumerables.

▶ **Th Charoen Krung** Starting on the western end of the street, near the intersection of Th Mahachai, is a collection of old record stores. **Talat Khlong Ong Ang** (Map 64, B1; 🚢Tha Ratchawong, Ⓜ Hua Lamphong exit 1 & taxi) consumes the next block, selling all sorts of used and new electronic gadgets. **Nakhon Kasem** (Map p64 C1; ⊙8am-8pm; 🚢Tha Saphan Phut) is the reformed thieves' market where vendors now stock up on gadgets for food prep. Further east, near Th Mahachak, is **Talat Khlong Thom** (Map p64, C2; 🚢Tha Ratchawong, Ⓜ Hua Lamphong exit 1 & taxi), a hardware centre.

▶ **Th Yaowarat** Chinatown's main drag is gold street, the biggest trading centre of the precious metal in the country. Near the intersection of Th Ratchawong, stores shift to Chinese and Singaporean tourists' tastes; the strip also retains a few Chinese apothecaries.

▶ **Th Mittraphan** (Map p64, E2) Signmakers branch off Wong Wian 22 Karakada; Thai and roman letters are typically cut out by a hand-guided lathe placed prominently beside the pavement.

▶ **Th Santiphap** (Map p64, D2) Car parts and other automotive gear make this the place for kicking tyres.

AUSTIN BUSH/GETTY IMAGES ©

Street food, Chinatown

Entertainment

Sala Chalermkrung THEATRE

15 ⭐ Map p64, B1

This art deco Bangkok landmark, a former cinema dating to 1933, is one of the few remaining places *kŏhn* can be witnessed. The traditional Thai dance-drama is enhanced here by laser graphics, hi-tech audio and English subtitles. Concerts and other events are also held; check the website for details. (📞0 2222 0434; www.salachal ermkrung.com; 66 Th Charoen Krung; tickets 800-1200B; ⏱shows 7.30pm Thu & Fri; 🛳Tha Saphan Phut (Memorial Bridge))

Cotton LIVE MUSIC

16 ⭐ Map p64, D3

Walk through a bland restaurant to this cosy retro-China-themed lounge in the Shanghai Mansion hotel. Virtually the only non-karaoke-based place of entertainment in Chinatown, Cotton features smooth acoustic jazz and affordable cocktails. (www.cotton.shang haimansion.com; 3rd fl, Shanghai Mansion, 479-481 Th Yaowarat; admission free; ⏱live music 6.30-10.30pm; 🛳Tha Ratchawong, Ⓜ Hua Lamphong exit 1 & taxi)

Explore

Siam Square, Pratunam & Ploenchit

Multistorey malls, department stores, open-air shopping precincts and seemingly never-ending markets leave no doubt that Siam Square, Pratunam and Ploenchit combine to form Bangkok's commercial district. The BTS (Skytrain) interchange at Siam has also made this area the de facto centre of today's Bangkok, so you'll probably find yourself here for touristing and dining as well as shopping.

The Sights in a Day

☀ Spend the morning taking in the architecture and antiques at **Jim Thompson's House** (p74). If contemporary art is more your thing, check out the latest exhibition at the nearby **Bangkok Art & Culture Centre** (p78).

☀ Cross over to the seven storeys of commerce that is **MBK Center** (p86), capping off your shopping spree with lunch at the cheap-but-tasty **MBK Food Court** (p82).

☾ Follow the elevated Sky Walk to the **Erawan Shrine** (p78), stopping along the way at **Siam Paragon** (p87), **Central World Plaza** (p88) and **Gaysorn Plaza** (p87). Consider a spa treatment at **Thann Sanctuary** (p79) or **Spa 1930** (p79), or cocktail treatment at **Hyde & Seek** (p83). Contrast your food-court lunch with a nouveau Thai dinner at **Sra Bua** (p80). If you've still got it in you, get boozy with the locals at **Co-Co Walk** (p85).

◉ **Top Sights**

Jim Thompson's House (p74)

♥ **Best of Bangkok**

Malls
MBK Center (p86)

Siam Square (p87)

Siam Paragon (p87)

Spas
Spa 1930 (p79)

Thann Sanctuary (p79)

For Kids
Siam Paragon (p87)

Siam Discovery Center (p89)

For Gay & Lesbian Travellers
Calypso Cabaret (p86)

Rooftop Bars
Red Sky (p85)

Street Eats
Food Plus (p82)

Getting There

Ⓢ Siam, National Stadium, Chit Lom, Phloen Chit, Ratchadamri

⚓ **Klorng boat** Tha Hua Chang, Tha Pratunam, Tha Chitlom, Tha Withayu

Top Sights
Jim Thompson's House

In 1959, 12 years after he singlehandedly turned Thai silk into a hugely successful export business, American Jim Thompson bought a piece of land and built himself a house. It wasn't, however, any old house. Thompson's love of all things Thai saw him buy six traditional wooden homes and re-construct them in his garden. Although he met a mysterious end in 1967, today Thompson's house remains, both as a museum to these unique structures and as a tribute to the man.

◉ Map p76, A2

www.jimthompsonhouse.com

6 Soi Kasem San 2

adult/child 100/50B

⊙ 9am-5pm

🚤 klorng boat to Tha Hua Chang, Ⓢ National Stadium exit 1

Jim Thompson's House

Don't Miss

The House

Thompson adapted his six buildings to create a larger home in which each room had a more familiar Western function. Another departure from tradition is the way Thompson arranged each wall with its exterior side facing the house's interior. Some of the homes were brought from the old royal capital of Ayuthaya; others were pulled down and floated across the canal.

Thompson's Art Collection

Thompson's small but splendid Asian art collection is also on display in the main house; pieces include rare Chinese porcelain and Burmese, Cambodian and Thai artefacts. Thompson had a particularly astute eye for somewhat less flashy but nonetheless charming objects, such as the 19th-century mouse maze that resembles a house.

The Grounds

After the tour, be sure to poke around the house's jungle-like gardens, which include a couple more structures that can be visited and ponds filled with exotic fish. The greater compound is also home to a cafe/restaurant and a shop flogging Jim Thompson–branded silk goods.

Jim Thompson Art Center

The compound also includes the **Jim Thompson Art Center** (admission free; ⊙9am-5pm), a museum with revolving displays spanning a variety of media; recent exhibitions have seen contributions from the likes of Palme d'Or–winning Thai filmmaker Apichatpong Weerasethakul.

☑ Top Tips

▶ Beware of well-dressed touts in soi near Jim Thompson's House who will tell you it is closed and then try to haul you off on a dodgy buying spree.

▶ The house can only be viewed via a guided tour, which is available in English, French and Thai.

▶ Photography is not allowed inside any of the buildings.

✕ Take a Break

On-site is the **Thompson Bar & Restaurant** (mains 160-480B; ⊙11am-11pm; ❄️✏️🏠), a convenient stop for a drink overlooking the garden or a Thai meal in air-con comfort. Otherwise, from Jim Thompson's House it's just a short walk to the MBK Food Court (p82), probably Bangkok's best.

A   **B**   **C**   **D**

26 🔾 Ⓢ Ratchathewi

Th Phetchaburi

21

🏧 36

Soi 12

Soi 18

Baan Krua 5 🔾

Jim Thompson's House 🔾

Tha Hua Chang

Th Phayathai

Khlong Saen Saeb

Sra Pathum Palace

9 ✕

Bangkok Art & Culture Centre

Soi Kasem San 2

Soi Kasem San 1

29 🔒

2 🔾

12 ✕

35 🔒

37 🔒

Ⓢ Siam

National Stadium

National Stadium Sporting Precinct

27 🔒

Soi 1

Soi 2

16 🔒

28 🔒

Siam

17 ✕

Soi 6

19 ✕

Th Phra Ram I

Soi 7

24 ✕

18 ✕

15 ✕

SIAM SQUARE

Soi Chulalongkorn 64

Th Chulalongkorn

Soi Chulalongkorn 5

Th Phayathai

Th Henri Dunant

PATHUMWAN

Royal Bangkok Sports Club

For reviews see

🔾 Top Sights   p74
🔾 Sights   p78
✕ Eating   p79
🔒 Drinking   p83
🏧 Entertainment   p86
🔒 Shopping   p86

E

34 🔒

Th Ratchaprarop

F

PRATUNAM

Soi Phetchaburi 31

G

Soi Phetchaburi 35

H

1

Th Phetchaburi

Tha 🚇
Pratunam

Tha 🚇
Chitlom

Lingam 🚇
Shrine 4

🚇 Tha
Withayu

2

Soi 32

Th Chitlom

Soi Somkhit

Th Witthayu (Wireless Rd)

23
🚇 🔒 32

Thann 6
Sanctuary ⊙ 🔒 30

33
🔒

Chit
Lom
Ⓢ

38
🔒

3

Erawan
Shrine ⊙ 1
❌ 8

Th Ploenchit

Phloen
Chit
Ⓢ

11
❌

13
❌ 22
31 🔒

20

Th Ratchadamri

❌ 10

Th Witthayu (Wireless Rd)

PLOENCHIT

4

Spa
1930 ⊙ 3

Ⓢ Ratchadamri

Soi Langsuan

Soi Tonson

Soi Ruam Rudi

Chalerm Mahanakhon Expwy

7
100 Tonson
Gallery ⊙

Soi 1

Soi 2

Soi 3

25 🍽

5

Ⓝ 0   500 m
  0   0.25 miles

❌ 14

Soi 4

Sights

Erawan Shrine   HINDU SHRINE

1 ◎ Map p76, E3

In Bangkok, commerce and religion are not mutually exclusive. This Brahman shrine was built after accidents delayed construction of the former Erawan Hotel (today the Grand Hyatt Erawan). News of the shrine's protective powers spread and merit makers now stream into the courtyard with their own petitions; commissioning a traditional Thai dance is a popular way of saying thanks if a wish was granted. (ศาลพระพรหม; cnr Th Ratchadamri & Th Ploenchit; admission free; ⊙6am-11pm; ⑤Chit Lom exit 8)

Bangkok Art & Culture Centre   ART GALLERY

2 ◎ Map p76, B2

This large, modern building in the centre of Bangkok is the most recent and promising addition to the city's arts scene. In addition to three floors and 3000 sq metres of gallery space, the centre also contains artsy shops, private galleries and cafes. Check the website to see what's on display when you're in town. (BACC; www.bacc.or.th; cnr Th Phayathai & Th Phra Ram 1; admission free; ⊙10am-9pm Tue-Sat; ⑤National Station exit 3)

EURASIA/GETTY IMAGES ©

Erawan Shrine

Spa 1930 SPA

3 ⊙ Map p76, F4

Discreet and sophisticated, Spa 1930 rescues relaxers from the contrived spa ambience of New Age music and ingredients you'd rather see at a dinner party. The menu is simple (face, body care and body massage) and the scrubs and massage oils are logical players. (☎0 2254 8606; www.spa1930.com; 42 Soi Tonson; à la carte from 1000B, packages 3500-3710B; ⊙9.30am-9.30pm; Ⓢ Chit Lom exit 4)

Lingam Shrine ANIMIST SHRINE

4 ⊙ Map p76, G2

This little shrine at the back of Swissôtel Nai Lert Park was built for the spirit of a tree. Soon word spread that the shrine had fertility powers and a small forest of wooden phalluses sprang up, creating one of Bangkok's bawdiest shrines. (ศาลเจ้าแม่ทับทิม; Swissôtel Nai Lert Park, Th Witthaya (Wireless Rd); admission free; ⊙24hr; 🚤klorng boat to Tha Withayu, Ⓢ Phloen Chit exit 1)

Baan Krua NEIGHBOURHOOD

5 ⊙ Map p76, A1

This neighbourhood dates back to the turbulent years at the end of the 18th century, when Muslims from Cambodia and Vietnam fought on the side of the new Thai king and were rewarded with this plot of land. The immigrants brought their silk-weaving traditions with them, and the community grew when the residents built the adjacent canal to better connect them to the river. Baan Krua is located north of Jim Thompon's House, just across Khlong Saen Saeb. (บ้านครัว; 🚤klorng boat to Tha Hua Chang, Ⓢ National Stadium exit 1)

Thann Sanctuary SPA

6 ⊙ Map p76, E3

This local brand of herbal-based soaps, lotions and cosmetics has launched a chain of mall-based spas – the perfect solution for post-shopping therapy. Also in Central World Plaza. (☎0 2658 0550; www.thann.info; 4th fl, Gaysorn Plaza, cnr Th Ploenchit & Th Ratchadamri; massage per hr 1800B, packages from 3200B; ⊙10am-9pm; Ⓢ Chit Lom exit 9)

100 Tonson Gallery ART GALLERY

7 ⊙ Map p76, F5

Housed in a spacious residential villa, and generally regarded as one of the city's top commercial galleries, 100 Tonson hosts a variety of contemporary exhibitions of all genres by local and international artists. (www.100tonsongallery.com; 100 Soi Tonson; ⊙11am-7pm Thu-Sun; Ⓢ Chit Lom exit 4)

Eating

Crystal Jade La Mian Xiao Long Bao CHINESE $$

8 ✗ Map p76, E3

The tongue-twistingly long name of this excellent Singaporean chain refers to the restaurant's signature *la mian* (wheat noodles) and the famous

Shanghainese *xiao long pao* ('soup' dumplings). If you order the hand-pulled noodles (which you should do), allow the staff to cut them with kitchen shears, otherwise you'll end up with ample evidence of your meal on your shirt. (Urban Kitchen, basement, Erawan Bangkok, 494 Th Ploenchit; mains 115-450B; ⏱11am-10pm; ❄🖊📷; Ⓢ Chit Lom exit 8)

Sra Bua   THAI $$$

9 ❌ Map p76, D2

Helmed by a Thai and a Dane whose Copenhagen restaurant snagged a Michelin star, Sra Bua takes a correspondingly international approach to Thai food. Putting Thai dishes and ingredients through the wringer of molecular gastronomy, the couple

have created dishes such as frozen red curry with lobster salad, and pomelo salad with grilled fish and warm yam sauce. (☎0 2162 9000; www.kempinski bangkok.com; ground fl, Siam Kempinski Hotel, 991/9 off Th Phra Ram I; set meal 1500-2400B; ⏱noon-3pm & 6-11pm; ❄📷; Ⓢ Siam exits 3 & 5)

Four Seasons
Sunday Brunch   INTERNATIONAL $$$

10 ❌ Map p76, E4

All of the Four Seasons' highly regarded restaurants – Spice Market, Shintaro, Biscotti and Madison – set up steam tables for this decadent Sunday brunch buffet. Numerous cooking stations and champagne options take this light years beyond your normal Sunday brunch. It's popular,

---

Understand
Jim Thompson

Born in Delaware in 1906, Jim Thompson served in a forerunner of the CIA in Thailand during WWII. When in 1947 he spotted some silk in a market and was told it was woven in Baan Krua, he found the only place in Bangkok where silk was still woven by hand. Thompson's Thai silk eventually attracted the interest of fashion houses in New York, Milan, London and Paris, and he gradually built a worldwide clientele for a craft that had been in danger of dying out.

In March of 1967 Thompson went missing while out for an afternoon walk in the Cameron Highlands of western Malaysia. Thompson has never been heard from since, but the conspiracy theories have never stopped. Was it communist spies? Business rivals? A man-eating tiger? Although the mystery has never been solved, evidence revealed by journalist Joshua Kurlantzick in his profile of Thompson, *The Ideal Man*, suggests that the vocal anti-American stance Thompson took later in his life may have made him a potential target of suppression by the CIA.

so be sure to reserve your table a couple of weeks in advance. (0 2250 1000; www.fourseasons.com/bangkok; ground fl, Four Seasons Hotel, 155 Th Ratchadamri; buffet 3178B; 11.30am-3pm Sun; ❄ 🍴 📶; ⑤ Ratchadamri exit 4)

Sanguan Sri
THAI $

11 🍴 Map p76, G3

This restaurant, essentially a concrete bunker filled with furniture circa 1973, can afford to remain decidedly cher-i (old-fashioned) simply because of its reputation. Mimic the area's hungry office staff and try central Thai dishes such as the excellent *gaang pèt Ђèt yâhng*, red curry with grilled duck breast served over snowy white rice noodles. No roman-script sign. (59/1 Th Witthayu (Wireless Rd); mains 40-150B; 10am-3pm Mon-Sat; ❄ 📶; ⑤ Phloen Chit exit 5)

Nuer Koo
THAI $

12 🍴 Map p76, C2

Is this the future of the noodle stall? Mall-bound Nuer Koo does an up-scale version of the formerly humble bowl of beef noodles. Choose your cut of beef – including Kobe beef from Japan – enjoy the rich broth and cool air-con, and quickly forget about the good old days. (4th fl, Siam Paragon, 991/1 Th Phra Ram I; mains 89-970B; 11.30am-9.30pm; ❄ 📶; ⑤ Siam exits 3 & 5)

✓ Top Tip
Living Large
In your home town you may be considered average or even petite, but in Thailand you're an extra large, clearly marked on the tag as 'XL'. If that batters the body image, then skip the street markets, where you'll bust the seams from the waist up. Instead, for formal wear, many expats turn to custom tailors, while many of the vendors at Pratunam Market (p88) and several stalls on the 7th floor of MBK Center (p86) stock larger sizes.

El Osíto
INTERNATIONAL $$

13 🍴 Map p76, H4

By day, El Osíto does deli-style sandwiches ranging from Reuben to banh mi; by night, the restaurant serves a menu of traditional and Latin American–inspired tapas dishes. Come during either shift and you can expect full-flavoured eats, an open loft-like feel and great drinks, including a selection of American craft beers. (www.facebook.com/ElOsitoBkk; 888/23-24 Mahatun Plaza, Th Ploenchit; mains 180-800B; 11.30am-3pm & 5-11pm; ❄ 📶; ⑤ Phloen Chit exits 2 & 4)

Gaggan
INDIAN $$$

14 🍴 Map p76, F5

The white, refurbished villa that houses Gaggan seems more appropriate for an English-themed teahouse than

Local Life
Dining on the Cheap

Admittedly, they tend to have all the ambience of a hospital cafeteria, but the mall-based food courts that abound in this part of town are among Bangkok's most user-friendly introductions to Thai food. They're cheap, clean and boast English-language menus. Our faves: **MBK Food Court** (Map p76, B2; 6th fl, MBK Center, cnr Th Phra Ram I & Th Phayathai; mains 35-150B; ⏱noon-9pm; ❄🌱📶; Ⓢ National Stadium exit 4), the biggest and best; **Gourmet Paradise** (Map p76, C2; ground fl, Siam Paragon, 991/1 Th Phra Ram I; mains 35-500B; ⏱10am-10pm; ❄📶; Ⓢ Siam exits 3 & 5), where you'll find branches of several 'famous' street vendors; and **FoodPark** (Map p76, E2; 4th fl, Big C, 97/11 Th Ratchadamri; mains 30-90B; ⏱9am-9pm; ❄📶; Ⓢ Chit Lom exit 9 to Sky Walk, Ⓢ Siam exit 6 to Sky Walk), a Thai food court for Thais.

a restaurant serving self-proclaimed 'progressive Indian', but Gaggan is all about incongruity. The set menu here spans 10 courses, ranging from the daring (a ball of raita) to the traditional (some excellent tandoori), with bright flavours and unexpected but satisfying twists as a unifying element. (📞0 2652 1700; www.eatatgaggan.com; 68/1 Soi Langsuan; set menu 1600B; ⏱noon-2.30pm & 6-11pm; ❄🌱📶; Ⓢ Ratchadamri exit 2)

Som Tam Nua   NORTHEASTERN THAI $

15 🍽 Map p76, C3

It can't compete with the street stalls for flavour or authenticity, but if you need to be seen, particularly while in air-con and trendy surroundings, this is a good place to sample northeastern Thai specialities. Expect a lengthy line at dinner. (392/14 Soi 5, Siam Sq; mains 59-130B; ⏱10.45am-9.30pm; ❄📶; Ⓢ Siam exit 4)

Koko   THAI $

16 🍽 Map p76, C3

Perfect for a mixed crowd; this casual cafe-like restaurant offers a lengthy veggie menu, not to mention a brief but solid repertoire of meat-based Thai dishes, such as a Penang curry served with tender pork, or fish deep-fried and served with Thai herbs. (262/2 Soi 3, Siam Sq; mains 70-220B; ⏱11am-9pm; ❄🌱📶; Ⓢ Siam exit 2)

Food Plus   THAI $

17 🍽 Map p76, C3

This claustrophobic alleyway is bursting with the wares of several *ráhn kôw gaang* (rice and curry stalls). Most dishes are made ahead of time, so simply point to what looks tasty. You'll be hard-pressed to spend more than 100B, and the flavours are unanimously authentic and tasty. (btwn Soi 5 & Soi 6, Siam Sq; mains 30-70B; ⏱9am-3pm; Ⓢ Siam exit 2)

New Light Coffee House

THAI-INTERNATIONAL **$**

18 Map p76, B3

Travel back in time to 1960s-era Bangkok at this vintage diner popular with students from nearby Chulalongkorn University. Try old-school Western dishes, all of which come accompanied by a soft roll and green salad, or choose from the extensive Thai menu. (426/1-4 Soi Chulalongkorn 64; mains 60-200B; ⊙8.30am-11.30pm; ✳ 🗋; S Siam exit 2)

Coca Suki

CHINESE-THAI **$$**

19 Map p76, D3

Immensely popular with Thai families, *sù·gêe* takes the form of a bubbling hotpot of broth and the raw ingredients to dip therein. Coca is one of the oldest purveyors of the dish, and this branch reflects the brand's efforts to appear more modern. Fans of spice be sure to request the tangy 'tom yam' broth. (416/3-8 Th Henri Dunant; mains 78-488B; ⊙11am-11pm; ✳ 🔧 🗋; S Siam exit 6)

Drinking

Hyde & Seek

BAR

20 🍷 Map p76, H4

The tasty and comforting English-inspired bar snacks and meals here have earned Hyde & Seek the right to call itself a 'gastro bar'. But we reckon

Nám đòk, a local spicy meat salad

GLENN SUNDEEN, TIGERPA/GETTY IMAGES ©

Understand

The Food of Bangkok

Geography, the influence of the royal palace and the Chinese and Muslim minorities have all pitched in to shape the local cuisine.

Central Thai Cuisine

The people of central Thailand are fond of sweet/savoury flavours, and many dishes include freshwater fish, pork, coconut milk and palm sugar. Central Thai eateries, particularly those in Bangkok, also serve a wide variety of seafood. Classic central Thai dishes include *yam blah dùk foo*, fried shredded catfish, chilli and peanuts served with a sweet/tart mango dressing, and *gaang sôm*, seafood, vegetables and/or herbs in a thick, tart broth.

Royal Thai Cuisine

A key influence on the city's kitchens has been the Bangkok-based royal court, which has been producing refined takes on central Thai dishes for nearly 300 years. Although previously available only within the palace walls, these so-called 'royal' Thai dishes can now be found across the city. One enduring example of royal cuisine is *mèe gròrp*, crispy noodles made the traditional way with a sweet/sour dressing.

Chinese-Thai Cuisine

Immigrants from southern China probably introduced the wok and several varieties of noodle dishes to Thailand. They also influenced Bangkok's cuisine in other ways: beef is not widely eaten in Bangkok due to a Chinese-Buddhist teaching that forbids eating 'large' animals. Perhaps the most common example of Thai-Chinese food is *kôw man gài*, Hainanese-style chicken rice.

Muslim-Thai Cuisine

Muslims are thought to have first visited Thailand during the late 14th century. They brought with them a cuisine based on meat and dried spices. While some Muslim dishes such as *roh·đee*, a fried bread similar to the Indian *paratha*, have changed little, if at all, others such as *gaang mát·sà·màn*, a rich curry, are a unique blend of Thai and Indian/Middle Eastern cooking styles and ingredients.

the real reasons to come are arguably Bangkok's best-stocked bar and some of the city's tastiest and most sophisticated cocktails. (ground fl, Athenee Residence, 65/1 Soi Ruam Rudi; ⊙11am-1am; **S**Phloen Chit exit 4)

Co-Co Walk
BAR

21 Map p76, B1

This covered compound is a smorgasbord of pubs, bars and live music popular with Thai university students. It's a fun, low-key place to drink like the locals do. (87/70 Th Phayathai; ⊙5pm-midnight; **S**Ratchathewi exit 2)

Ad Makers
BAR

22 Map p76, H4

The most recent incarnation of this mature-feeling bar-restaurant – originally started up in 1985 by a group of ad-executive buddies – draws in diners and partiers with tasty regional Thai eats, live tunes (from Tuesday to Saturday) and draught beer. (ground fl, Athenee Residence, 65/1 Soi Ruam Rudi; ⊙11am-2pm & 5pm-1am Mon-Fri, 5pm-1am Sat & Sun; **S**Phloen Chit exit 4)

Red Sky
BAR

23 Map p76, E3

Perched on the 55th floor of a sleek skyscraper, Bangkok's newest rooftop venture feels a bit more formal than most and, as such, boasts an extensive wine list and a martini menu. As is the case with most of Bangkok's rooftop bars, those wearing shorts and/or sandals aren't invited to the party. (55th fl, Centara Grand, Central World Plaza; ⊙5pm-1am; **S**Chit Lom exit 9 to Sky Walk, Siam exit 6 to Sky Walk)

To-Sit
BAR

24 Map p76, C3

Live, loud and sappy music; cheap and spicy food; good friends and cold beer: To-Sit epitomises everything a Thai university student could wish for on a night out. There are branches all over town (check the website), but the Siam Sq location has the advantage of being virtually the only option in an area that's buzzing during the day but dead at night. (www.tosit.com; Soi 3, Siam Sq; **S**Siam exit 2)

Siam Square (p87)

Siam Paragon

Diplomat Bar
BAR

25 Map p76, G5

Named for its location in the middle of the embassy district, this is one of the few hotel lounges that locals make a point of visiting. Choose from an expansive list of innovative martinis and sip to live jazz, played gracefully at conversation level. (ground fl, Conrad Hotel, 87 Th Witthayu (Wireless Rd); ⊙5pm–1am; ⑤Phloen Chit exit 5)

Entertainment

Calypso Cabaret
THEATRE

26 Map p76, B1

Watching gà·teu·i (transgender people; also spelt kàthoey) perform tacky show tunes has, not surprisingly, become the latest 'must-do' fixture on the Bangkok tourist circuit. Calypso caters to the trend with choreographed stage shows featuring Broadway high kicks and lip-synched pop tunes. (☏0 2653 3960; www.calypso cabaret.com; Asia Hotel, 296 Th Phayathai; adult/child 1200/600B; ⊙show times 8.15pm & 9.45pm; ⑤Ratchathewi exit 1)

Shopping

MBK Center
SHOPPING CENTRE

27 Map p76, B3

This immense shopping mall is quickly becoming one of Bangkok's top attractions. Swedish and other foreign languages can be heard as much as

Thai, and on any given weekend half of Bangkok can be found here combing through an inexhaustible range of stalls and shops stocking mobile phones, accessories, shoes, camera equipment, handbags and T-shirts. (www.mbk-center.com; cnr Th Phra Ram I & Th Phayathai; ⏱10am-10pm; **S**National Stadium exit 4)

Siam Square   SHOPPING CENTRE

28 🔒 Map p76, C3

Siam Square is ground zero for teenage culture in Bangkok. Pop music blares out of tinny speakers, and gangs of hipsters in various costumes ricochet between fast-food restaurants and closet-sized boutiques. Several shops peddle pop-hip styles along Soi 2 and Soi 3, but most outfits require a 'barely there' waist. (Th Phra Ram I; ⏱11am-9pm; **S**Siam exits 2, 4 & 6)

Siam Paragon   SHOPPING CENTRE

29 🔒 Map p76, C2

Paragon epitomises the city's fanaticism for the new, the excessive, and absurd slogans. In addition to the usual high-end brands, you'll find a buzzing basement-level food court; the 3rd floor Kinokuniya, Bangkok's best-stocked bookshop; and on the same floor, the True Urban Park 'lifestyle centre', featuring a cafe, internet access and a shop selling books, music and camera equipment. (www.siamparagon.co.th; 991/1 Th Phra Ram I; ⏱10am-10pm; **S**Siam exits 3 & 5)

Gaysorn Plaza   SHOPPING CENTRE

30 🔒 Map p76, E3

This fashion palace accommodates all the haughty international designers and Thai high-flyers, not to mention a top floor that is one of Bangkok's best one-stop shopping destinations for high-end home decor, the highlights of which include the eclectic D&O Shop, the fragrant soaps at Thann and the Asian-influenced ceramics at Lamont. (www.gaysorn.com; cnr Th Ploenchit & Th Ratchadamri; ⏱10am-8pm; **S**Chit Lom exit 9)

Local Life
Siam Square's Silver Screens

The Siam Sq area is home to Bangkok's ritziest cinemas. Each mall has its own theatre, but **Siam Paragon Cineplex** (Map p76, C2; ☎0 2129 4635; www.paragoncineplex.com; 5th fl, Siam Paragon, 991/1 Th Phra Ram I; **S**Siam exits 3 & 5), with 16 screens (including an IMAX theatre) and 5000 seats, comes out on top. For something with a bit more character, consider the old-school stand-alone theatres just across the street such as **Scala** (Map p76, B3; ☎0 2251 2861; Soi 1, Siam Sq; **S**Siam exit 2) and **Lido** (Map p76, C3; ☎0 2252 6498; www.apexsiamsquare.com; btwn Soi 2 & Soi 3, Siam Sq; **S**Siam exit 2).

Pinky Tailors
TAILOR

31 Map p76, H4

Suit jackets have been Mr Pinky's spe-ciality for 35 years. His custom-made dress shirts, for both men and women, also have dedicated fans. Located behind the Mahatun Building. (www.pinkytailor.com; 888/40 Mahatun Plaza, Th Ploenchit; ⏱10am-7pm Mon-Sat; ⓢPhloen Chit exits 2 & 4)

Central World Plaza
SHOPPING CENTRE

32 Map p76, E3

Spanning eight storeys of more than 500 shops and 100 restaurants, Central World is one of Southeast Asia's largest shopping centres. But it suffered a huge setback in May 2010 when its centrepiece Zen department store was torched by fleeing protesters. Other parts of the complex were largely unaf-fected, and in 2012, Zen was finally reopened. (www.centralworld.co.th; Th Ratchadamri; ⏱10am-10pm; ⓢChit Lom exit 9 to Sky Walk, Siam exit 6 to Sky Walk)

Narai Phand
SOUVENIRS

33 Map p76, E3

Souvenir-quality handicrafts are given fixed prices and comfortable air-conditioning at this government-run facility. You won't find anything here that you haven't already seen at all of the tourist street markets, but it is a good stop if you're pressed for time or are spooked by haggling. (www.naraiphand.com; ground fl, President Tower, 973 Th Ploenchit; ⏱10am-8pm; ⓢChit Lom exit 7)

Pratunam Market
CLOTHING, MARKET

34 Map p76, E1

The emphasis here is on cheap clothes, and you could spend hours flipping through the T-shirts at the seemingly endless Baiyoke Garment Center, but it doesn't end there: across the street is the five-storey Platinum Fashion Mall, which sports the latest in no-brand couture. (cnr Th Phetchaburi

& Th Ratchaprarop; ⏱10am-10pm; 🚤klorng boat to Tha Pratunam, Ⓢ Chit Lom exit 9)

Siam Center
SHOPPING CENTRE

35 🔒 Map p76, C2

Siam Center, Thailand's first shopping centre, was built in 1976 but, since a recent nip and tuck, it hardly shows its age. Its 3rd floor is one of the best locations to check out established local labels such as Flynow, Senada Theory and Tango. (cnr Th Phra Ram I & Th Phayathai, Siam Sq; ⏱10am-9pm; Ⓢ Siam exit 1)

Pantip Plaza
SHOPPING CENTRE

36 🔒 Map p76, D1

If you can tolerate the crowds and annoying pornography vendors ('DVD sex? DVD sex?'), Pantip, a multistorey computer and electronics warehouse, might just be your kinda paradise. Technocrati will find pirated software and music, gear for hobbyists to enhance their machines, flea market–

style peripherals and other odds and ends. (604 Th Phetchaburi; ⏱10am-9pm; Ⓢ Ratchathewi exit 4)

Siam Discovery Center
SHOPPING CENTRE

37 🔒 Map p76, B2

A modern mall, right in the centre of mall-land, with a few interesting domestic outlets such as Doi Tung and Propaganda. Kids will be fascinated by the branch of Madam Tussaud's. (cnr Th Phra Ram I & Th Phayathai, Siam Sq; ⏱10am-9pm; Ⓢ Siam exit 1)

Central Chidlom
SHOPPING CENTRE

38 🔒 Map p76, F3

Central is a modern Western-style department store with locations throughout the city. This flagship store, Thailand's largest, is the snazziest of all the branches. (www.central.co.th; 1027 Th Ploenchit; ⏱10am-10pm; Ⓢ Chit Lom exit 5)

Local Life
Victory Monument

Getting There

S BTS Phaya Thai and Victory Monument

For a glimpse of Bangkok without the touts, tourists or malls (well, OK, there are some malls – this is, after all, Bangkok), take the BTS north to the Victory Monument, where you'll find ordinary Thais doing ordinary Thai things, not to mention a handful of worthwhile attractions, good restaurants and fun bars.

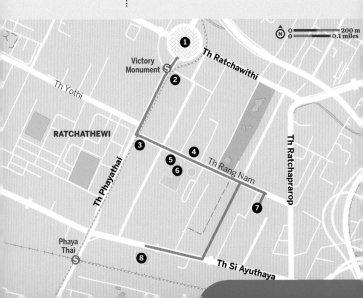

1 Victory Monument

The obelisk **Victory Monument** (อนุสาวรีย์ชัย; cnr Th Ratchawithi & Th Phayathai; admission free; [S] Victory Monument) was built by the then military government in 1941 to commemorate a 1940 campaign against the French in Laos.

2 Saxophone Pub & Restaurant

After all these years, **Saxophone** (www.saxophonepub.com; 3/8 Th Phayathai; ⊙7.30pm-1.30am; [S] Victory Monument exit 2) remains Bangkok's premier live-music venue – a dark, intimate space where you can pull up a chair just a few metres away from the band and see their every bead of sweat.

3 Sky Train Jazz Club

The **Sky Train Jazz Club** (cnr Th Rang Nam & Th Phayathai; ⊙5pm-2am; [S] Victory Monument exit 2) is more like the rooftop of your stoner buddy's flat than any jazz club we've ever been to. But that's what makes it so fun. To find it, look for the sign and proceed up the graffiti-covered stairway until you reach the roof.

4 Mallika Restaurant

Visit **Mallika** (21/36 Th Rang Nam; mains 130-550B; ⊙10am-10pm; ❄; [S] Victory Monument exit 2) for a taste of Thailand's southern provinces. The menu spans the region with spicy hits such as *kôo·a glîng* (here called 'southern-style stir fry') or *gaang sôm* (a turmeric-laden seafood soup). Prices are slightly higher than elsewhere, but you're paying for quality.

5 Aksra Theatre

A variety of shows are held at **Aksra Theatre** (☎0 2677 8888, ext 5730; www.aksratheatre.com; 3rd fl, King Power Complex, 8/1 Th Rang Nam; tickets 499-599B; ⊙shows 12.30pm & 6.30pm; [S] Victory Monument exit 2), but the highlight is performances of the *Ramakian* using knee-high puppets that require three puppeteers. Performances include a buffet meal.

6 Wine Pub

If the upmarket but chilled setting and DJ aren't reason enough to visit **Wine Pub** (www.pullmanbangkokkingpower; 1st fl, Pullman Bangkok King Power, 8/2 Th Rang Nam; ⊙6pm-2am; [S] Victory Monument exit 2), the fact that it's one of the cheapest places in Bangkok to drink wine and nibble imported cheeses and cold cuts are.

7 Raintree

Raintree (116/63-64 Th Rang Nam; ⊙8pm-2am; [S] Victory Monument exit 2) is one of the few remaining places in town to host 'songs for life', Thai folk music with roots in the communist insurgency of the 1960s and '70s. Tasty bar snacks also make it a clever place to eat.

8 Suan Pakkad Palace Museum

Suan Pakkad (วังสวนผักกาด; Th Si Ayuthaya; admission 100B; ⊙9am-4pm; [S] Phaya Thai exit 4) is eight traditional wooden Thai houses. Within the stilt buildings are displays of art, antiques and furnishings. The landscaped grounds are a peaceful oasis in an otherwise urban area.

Explore

Riverside, Silom & Lumphini

Although you may not see it behind the office blocks, high-rise condos and hotels, Mae Nam Chao Phraya (the Chao Phraya River) forms a watery backdrop to these linked neighbourhoods. History is still palpable in the riverside area's crumbling architecture, while heading inland, Silom, Bangkok's de facto financial district, is frenetic and modern, and adjacent Lumphini is the city's green lungs.

The Sights in a Day

☀ If you're a morning person – or still find yourself jet-lagged – get an early start on the day at **Lumphini Park** (p98). Follow this with a visit to the quirky antivenin factory that is the **Queen Saovabha Memorial Institute** (p99).

☀ Lunch on the famous fried chicken at **Kai Thort Jay Kee** (p102). Pop into **Sri Mariamman Temple** (p100) followed by a look at the latest photography exhibition at **Kathmandu Photo Gallery** (p98). Spend the remainder of the afternoon window-shopping for antiques at **House of Chao** (p108) and **River City** (p108).

☾ Have a sunset cocktail at **viva aviv** (p106) then board a ship for a **dinner cruise** (p104) along Mae Nam Chao Phraya. Alternatively, head inland and down a rooftop cocktail at **Moon Bar** (p105) followed by dinner at **nahm** (p101), the latter home to some of the best Thai food in Bangkok.

For a local's gay evening in Silom, see p94.

🔍 **Local Life**

Gay Silom (p94)

💜 **Best of Bangkok**

Rooftop Bars
Moon Bar (p105)

Sirocco Sky Bar (p106)

Foreign Cuisine Dining
D'sens (p102)

Zanotti (p103)

Shopping
River City (p108)

Thai Massage
Ruen-Nuad Massage Studio (p98)

Health Land (p99)

Museums
Bangkokian Museum (p98)

Dance Clubs
Tapas Room (p105)

Getting There

🚊 **S** Sala Daeng, Ratchadamri, Chong Nonsi, Surasak and Saphan Taksin

M Si Lom and Lumphini

🛥 **River ferry** Tha Si Phraya, Tha Oriental and Tha Sathon

Local Life
Gay Silom

The side streets off lower Th Silom are so gay that they make San Francisco look like rural Texas. In addition to heaps of gay locals and tourists, the area is also home to a smattering of massage parlours and saunas, the in-your-face sex shows in nearby Duangthawee Plaza, the chilled open-air bars on Soi 4 and the clubs near Soi 2.

① Telephone & Balcony

Commence your evening on Soi 4, arguably Bangkok's pinkest street. It's home to predominantly gay shops, bars, clubs and restaurants. The best views of the action are from long-standing streetside bars **Telephone Pub** (www.telephonepub.com; 114/11-13 Soi 4, Th Silom; ⊙6pm-1am; ⊛; Ⓜ Si Lom exit 2, Ⓢ Sala Daeng exit 1) and, directly across the street, **Balcony** (www.balconypub.com;

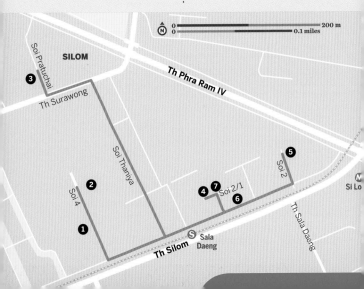

86-88 Soi 4, Th Silom; ⏰5.30pm-1am; 📶; Ⓜ️Si Lom exit 2, Ⓢ Sala Daeng exit 1).

❷ Bearbie

A bear bar as perceived through the Thai lens, **Bearbie** (2nd fl, 82 Soi 4, Th Silom; ⏰8pm-1am Tue-Thu, to 2am Fri-Sun; Ⓜ️Si Lom exit 2, Ⓢ Sala Daeng exit 1) replaces beards and bikers with local 'chubs' and teddy bear-themed karaoke rooms. Check its Facebook page to see what events are lined up.

❸ Duangthawee Plaza

Finding the Soi 4 scene a tad too tame? Cross over to **Duangthawee Plaza** (Soi Twilight; Soi Pratuchai; ⏰7pm-1am; Ⓜ️Si Lom exit 2, Ⓢ Sala Daeng exit 3), a strip of male-only go-go bars (sample names: Hot Male, Fresh Beach Boy, Dream Boy) that is the gay equivalent of nearby Th Patpong. Expect tacky sex shows performed by bored-looking boys.

❹ Men Factory

If you're into the sauna scene, there are a few options in this part of town. **Men Factory** (www.mfsauna.com; Soi 2/1, Th Silom; admission 150-170B; ⏰2pm-6am; Ⓜ️Si Lom exit 2, Ⓢ Sala Daeng exit 1) is a newish place that offers the entire spectrum of options, from Thai massage on a daily basis to nude nights on Wednesday, Friday and Sunday.

❺ DJ Station

DJ Station (www.dj-station.com; 8/6-8 Soi 2, Th Silom; ⏰10.30pm-3am; Ⓜ️Si Lom exit 2, Ⓢ Sala Daeng exit 1) is one of Bangkok's most legendary gay dance clubs. Get there at 11.30pm for the nightly cabaret show, or later for a packed house of Thai guppies (gay professionals), money boys and a few Westerners. There are several similar dance clubs and bars crammed into this tiny street. Admission 100B to 200B.

❻ Coffee Society

Take a breather, fuel up, or simply partake in one of the area's more low-key gay scenes at **Coffee Society** (12/3 Th Silom; ⏰24hr; 📶; Ⓜ️Si Lom exit 2, Ⓢ Sala Daeng exit 1), a casual cafe/restaurant that never closes.

❼ G Bangkok

Three floors barely supporting one of Bangkok's better DJs and a partying, mostly muscly/expat crowd, **G Bangkok** (Guys on Display; Soi 2/1, Th Silom; ⏰8pm-late; Ⓜ️Si Lom exit 2, Ⓢ Sala Daeng exit 1) is where to go after DJ Station (and just about every other bar in town) has already closed. Admission 300B.

A

TALAT NOI
Soi 22

1

Tha Marine
Department

Sam Yan **M**

D

Th Sri Phraya

SaphanT ia

Soi Sawang

Th Maha Phrutharam

Th Maha Nakhon

Th Yotha

B

C

42
40

River
City
Pier **30**

Tha Si
Phraya

Th Si Phraya

Soi 39

Soi 30

Soi 41

Soi 43

Bangkokian
Museum
2

BANGRAK

Neilson
Hays
Library

13

Th Naret

Soi 1

Th Surawong

24

Th Sap

2

Soi 32

Soi 34

Th Mahesak

Soi 20 (Soi Pradit)

Soi 24

Soi 18

Soi 16

Soi 14

Th Decho

39

Th Silom

3

Oriental
Spa **9**
37

Mae Nam Chao Phraya

Soi 36
19
36
46 44
45
Soi 40
26
Soi 42
Soi 36

Tha
Oriental

31

Soi 44
Soi 46
48

Soi 34 – Bangkok Expwy
Phayathai

Soi 21

Th Surasak

Soi 30

Soi 32

Soi 28

Soi 26

Silom
Galleria
10

Soi 19

21

23

Th Pramuan

Soi Si Wiang

Sri Mariamman
Temple
7
18

Soi 11

Kathmandu
Photo
Gallery **3**

Th Pan

12
H Gallery
Health Lan

Soi 12

Soi 10

6

4

Saphan
Taksin

**Saphan
Taksin** **S**

Tha Sathon
(Central
Pier)

Th Charoen Krung

Soi 50

Th Sathon Neua (North)

S Surasak

Th Sathon Tai (South)

Soi St Louis 2

Soi St Louis 3

Soi Pi
Soi
Pich

5

Soi St Louis 2

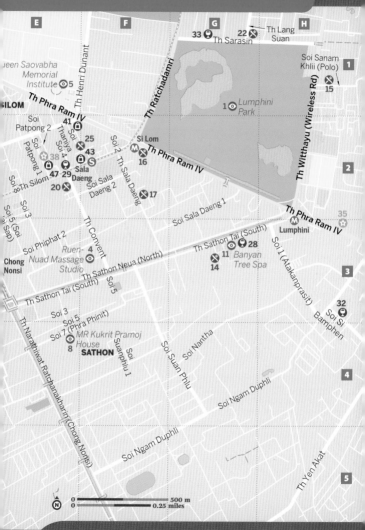

E

F

G
33 🏛

22 ✕ Th Lang
Th Sarasin Suan

H

ueen Saovabha
Memorial
Institute ◉ 5

Th Henri Dunant

Th Ratchadamri

Soi Sanam
Khlii (Polo)

1

✕ 15

ILOM

Th Phra Ram IV

1 ◉ Lumphini
Park

Th Witthayu (Wireless Rd)

Soi
Patpong 2

Soi Patpong 1

Thaniya
Soi 4

41

25

Soi 2

Si Lom

43

Th Sala Daeng

M
16

Th Phra Ram IV

🏛 38
47 29

S
Sala
Daeng

Soi Sala
Daeng 2

20 ✕

Soi Th Silom

2

✕ 17

Soi 5 (Soi
Sap)

Soi 3

Th Convent

Soi Sala Daeng 1

Th Phra Ram IV

M
Lumphini

35

2

Soi Phiphat 2

Ruen- 4
Nuad Massage ◉
Studio

Th Sathon Tai (South)

🍴 28
11

Chong
Nonsi

Th Sathon Neua (North)

Soi 5

✕ 14

Banyan
Tree Spa

Soi 1 (Atakanprasit)

3

Th Sathon Tai (South)

Th Narathiwat Ratchanakharin (Chong Nonsi)

Soi 3

Soi 5

Soi 7 (Phra Phinit)

MR Kukrit Pramoj ◉
House
8 SATHON

Soi
Suanphlu 1

Soi Suan Phlu

Soi Nantha

32
🏛

Soi Si
Bamphen

3

4

Soi Ngam Duphli

Soi Ngam Duphli

Th Yen Akat

5

Ⓝ

0   500 m
0   0.25 miles

Sights

Lumphini Park
PARK

1 Map p96, G1

Named after the Buddha's birthplace in Nepal, central Bangkok's biggest and most popular park has nurtured many a bike rider, jogger, *dà-grôr* (a Thai ball game) player and t'ai chi practitioner – all best observed during the cool morning hours. Likewise, keep your eyes open for the enormous urban monitor lizards. (สวนลุมพินี; bounded by Th Sarasin, Th Phra Ram IV, Th Witthayu (Wireless Rd) & Th Ratchadamri; ⏱4.30am-9pm; Ⓜ Lumphini exit 3, Si Lom exit 1, Ⓢ Sala Daeng exit 3, Ratchadamri exit 2)

☑ Top Tip

Hotel Boats

Getting out on Mae Nam Chao Phraya is a great way to escape Bangkok's notorious traffic and experience the city's maritime past. So it's fortunate that the city's riverside hotels also have some of the most attractive boats shuttling along the river (technically for hotel guests, but staff don't generally ask too many questions). In most cases these free services run from Tha Sathon (also known as Central Pier) to their mother hotel, departing every 10 or 15 minutes. There's no squeeze, no charge and a uniformed crew will help you on and off.

Bangkokian Museum
MUSEUM

2 Map p96, B2

This collection of three wooden houses illustrates an often-overlooked period of Bangkok's history, the 1950s and '60s. The grounds consist of two handsome wooden homes, both of which are decked out with their original furniture, and an adjacent museum dedicated to local history. A visit takes the form of an informal guided tour in halting English, and photography is encouraged. (พิพิธภัณฑ์ชาวบางกอก; 273 Soi 43, Th Charoen Krung; admission free; ⏱10am-4pm Wed-Sun; 🚢 Tha Si Phraya)

Kathmandu Photo Gallery
ART GALLERY

3 Map p96, C3

Bangkok's only gallery wholly dedicated to photography is housed in an attractively restored Sino-Portuguese shophouse. The work of the owner, acclaimed Thai photographer Manit Sriwanichpoom, is on display on the ground floor, and the small but airy upstairs gallery plays host to changing exhibitions by local and international shooters. (www.kathmandu-bkk.com; 87 Th Pan; admission free; ⏱11am-7pm Tue-Sun; Ⓢ Surasak exit 3)

Ruen-Nuad Massage Studio
MASSAGE

4 Map p96, F3

Set in a refurbished wooden house, this charming place successfully skirts

Kathmandu Photo Gallery

both the tackiness and New Age style that characterise most Bangkok massage joints. Prices are approachable, too. (🕿 0 2632 2662; 42 Th Convent; Thai massage per hr 350B; ⊙10am-9.30pm; Ⓜ Si Lom exit 2, Ⓢ Sala Daeng exit 2)

Queen Saovabha Memorial Institute

FARM

5 ◉ Map p96, E1

This snake farm, one of only a few worldwide, was established in 1923 to breed snakes for antivenins. There's a small museum dedicated to snakes, while venom is collected during daily milkings (11am Monday to Friday), and daily snake-handling performances (2.30pm Monday to Friday, 11am Saturday and Sunday) are held at the outdoor amphitheatre. (สถานเสาวภา, Snake Farm; cnr Th Phra Ram IV & Th Henri Dunant; adult/child 200/50B; ⊙9.30am-3.30pm Mon-Fri, to 1pm Sat & Sun; Ⓜ Si Lom exit 1, Ⓢ Sala Daeng exit 3)

Health Land

SPA

6 ◉ Map p96, D4

This, the main branch of a longstanding Thai massage mini-empire, offers good-value, no-nonsense massage and spa treatments in a tidy environment. It's popular, so be sure to book your treatment or massage at least a day in advance. (🕿 0 2637 8883; www.healthlandspa.com; 120 Th Sathon Neua; Thai massage 2hr 450B; ⊙9am-midnight; Ⓢ Surasak exit 3)

Sri Mariamman Temple

HINDU TEMPLE

7 ◉ Map p96, C3

Built by Tamil immigrants in the 1860s, this Hindu temple is a colourful place of worship in every sense of the word, from the multihued main temple to the eclectic range of people of many faiths and ethnicities who come here to make offerings. Thais often call it Wat Khaek – *kàak* being a common expression for people of Indian descent. (วัดพระศรีมหาอุมาเทวี (วัดแขก), Wat Phra Si Maha Umathewi; cnr Th Silom & Th Pan; admission free; ◷6am-8pm; ⓈSurasak exit 3)

MR Kukrit Pramoj House

MUSEUM

8 ◉ Map p96, E4

Former Thai prime minister Mom Ratchawong Kukrit Pramoj once lived in this beautiful garden compound that today is open to visitors. European-educated but devoutly Thai, MR Kukrit surrounded himself with the best of both worlds: five traditional teak buildings, Thai art, Western books and lots of heady conversations. (บ้านหม่อม ราชวงศ์คึกฤทธิ์ปราโมช; Soi 7 (Phra Phinit), Th Narathiwat Ratchanakharin; adult/child 50/20B; ◷10am-4pm; ⓈChong Nonsi exit 2)

Oriental Spa

SPA

9 ◉ Map p96, A3

Regarded as among the premier spas in the world, the Oriental Spa also sets the standard for Asian-style spa treatment. Depending on where you flew in from, the jet-lag massage might be a good option, but all treatments require advance booking. The spa is located opposite the hotel, across the Mae Nam Chao Phraya, and is accessible via a hotel shuttle boat. (☏0 2659 9000; www.mandarinoriental.com/bangkok/spa; Mandarin Oriental, 48 Soi 40, Th Charoen Krung; spa packages from 2900B; ◷9am-10pm; 🚢Tha Oriental or hotel shuttle boat from Tha Sathon (Central Pier))

Silom Galleria

ART GALLERY

10 ◉ Map p96, B3

The only reason to visit this rather empty-feeling art- and jewellery-focussed shopping centre is for a

JEAN-PIERRE LESCOURRET/GETTY IMAGES ©

T'ai Chi in Lumphini Park (p98)

peek into two of Bangkok's better commercial art galleries. Tang Gallery has a distinct emphasis on works by new and established Chinese artists, while Number 1 Gallery focuses on contemporary Thai art. (919/1 Th Silom; ⏰6am-10pm; Ⓢ Surasak exit 3)

Banyan Tree Spa SPA

11 ⊚ Map p96, G3

This 21st-floor spa is one of the most luxurious in the city. Decked out in new-millennium tranquillity, the spa uses deep-tissue massages, body wraps in warming spices and a flower bath to transport you further into the beyond. (🖉0 2679 1052; www.banyantreespa .com; 21/100 Th Sathon Tai; massage packages from 3200B; ⏰9am-10pm; Ⓜ Lumphini)

H Gallery ART GALLERY

12 ⊚ Map p96, D3

Housed in a refurbished colonial-era wooden building, H is generally considered among the city's leading private galleries. It is also seen as a jumping-off point for Thai artists with international ambitions, such as Jakkai Siributr and Somboon Hormthienthong. (www.hgallerybkk.com; 201 Soi 12, Th Sathon Neua; ⏰10am-6pm Wed-Sat, by appointment Tue; Ⓢ Chong Nonsi exit 1)

Neilson Hays Library LIBRARY

13 ⊚ Map p96, C2

The oldest English-language library in Thailand, the Neilson Hays dates back to 1922, and today remains the city's

☑ Top Tip

Art Attack

Bangkok is home to an ever-expanding network of private art galleries. To keep tabs, or see what recommended exhibitions are on during your stay, check out the **Bangkok Art Map** (www.bangkok artmap.com).

noblest place for a read – with the added benefit of air-con. It has a good selection of children's books and a decent selection of titles on Thailand. Nonmembers are expected to pay a 50B fee to use the facilities. (www.neil sonhayslibrary.com; 195 Th Surawong; family membership 3300B; ⏰9.30am-5pm Tue-Sun; Ⓢ Surasak exit 3)

Eating

nahm THAI $$$

14 ✕ Map p96, G3

Australian chef-author David Thompson is behind what is quite possibly the best Thai restaurant in Bangkok. Using ancient cookbooks as his inspiration, Thompson has given new life to previously extinct dishes such as smoked fish curry with prawns, chicken livers, cockles and black pepper. If you're expecting bland, gentrified Thai food meant for foreigners, prepare to be disappointed. Reservations recommended. (🖉0 2625 3388; www.comohotels.com/

metropolitanbangkok/dining/nahm; ground fl, Metropolitan Hotel, 27 Th Sathon Tai; set lunch 800-1100B, set dinner 1700B; ⊘noon-2pm Mon-Fri & 7-10.30pm Mon-Sun; ❄ 🗋; Ⓜ Lumphini exit 2)

Kai Thort Jay Kee   THAI $

15 🍴 Map p96, H1

Although the *sôm·dam* (papaya salad), sticky rice and *lâhp* (spicy 'salad' of minced meat) give the impression of an northeastern Thai eatery, the restaurant's namesake deep-fried bird is more southern in origin. Regardless, smothered in a thick layer of crispy deep-fried garlic, it is none other than a truly Bangkok experience. (Soi Polo Fried Chicken; 137/1-3 Soi Sanam Khlii

(Polo); mains 40-280B; ⊘11am-9pm; ❄ 🗋; Ⓜ Lumphini exit 3)

D'sens   FRENCH $$$

16 🍴 Map p96, F2

Atop the Dusit Thani, overlooking Lumphini Park, this is a venture of French wonder-twins Laurent and Jacques Pourcel, creators of the Michelin-starred Le Jardin des Sens in Montpellier, France. One of Bangkok's best fine-dining options, the restaurant is handsome yet modern and, likewise, features a progressive menu that draws from the traditions of the south of France. (📞 0 2200 9000; www.dusit.com; 22nd fl, Dusit Thani Hotel, 946 Th Phra Ram IV; set lunch 950B, set

Queen Saovabha Memorial Institute (p99)

dinner 3100B; ⏰11.30am-2pm & 6-10pm Mon-Fri, 6-10pm Sat; ✱ 🔅; Ⓜ Si Lom exit 3, Ⓢ Sala Daeng exit 4)

Zanotti
ITALIAN $$$

17 🍴 Map p96, F2

Zanotti has a well-deserved reputation as one of Bangkok's best destinations for Italian. Much of this is due to the menu, which is packed with satisfying meaty pasta and rice dishes. But we also fancy the dark wood and framed paintings of the gentlemen's club–like dining room, not to mention the professional and confident service, a rarity in Bangkok. (www.zanottigroup .com; 21/2 Th Sala Daeng; mains 200-1200B; ⏰11.30am-2pm & 6-10.30pm; ✱ 🔅; Ⓜ Si Lom exit 3, Ⓢ Sala Daeng exit 4)

Chennai Kitchen
INDIAN-VEGETARIAN $

18 🍴 Map p96, C3

This thimble-sized mom-and-pop restaurant near the Hindu temple puts out some of the most solid southern Indian vegetarian food around. Yard-long *dosai* (a crispy southern Indian bread) is always a good choice, but if you're feeling indecisive (or exceptionally famished) go for the banana-leaf thali, which seems to incorporate just about everything in the kitchen. (10 Th Pan; mains 70-150B; ⏰10am-3pm & 6-9pm; ✱ 🖋 🔅; Ⓢ Surasak exit 3)

Le Normandie
FRENCH $$$

19 🍴 Map p96, A3

For decades Le Normandie has been synonymous with fine dining in Bangkok. A revolving cast of Michelin-starred guest chefs and some of the world's most decadent ingredients keep up the standard, and appropriately, formal attire (including jacket) is required. Book ahead. (📞0 2236 0400; www.mandarin oriental.com; Mandarin Oriental Hotel, Soi 40, Th Charoen Krung; mains 1100-3750B; ⏰noon-2.30pm & 7-11pm Mon-Sat, 7-11pm Sun; Tha Oriental or hotel shuttle boat from Tha Sathon (Central Pier))

Somtam Convent
NORTHEASTERN THAI $

20 🍴 Map p96, E2

Northeastern-style Thai food is usually relegated to less-than-hygienic stalls perched by the side of the road with no menu or English-speaking staff in sight. A less intimidating introduction to the wonders of *lâhp* (a minced meat 'salad'), *sôm·dam* (papaya salad) and other rustic delights can be had at this popular restaurant. (Hai; 2/4-5 Th Convent; mains 30-100B; ⏰10am-9pm Mon-Fri, to 5pm Sat; 🔅; Ⓜ Si Lom exit 2, Ⓢ Sala Daeng exit 2)

Taling Pling
THAI $

21 🍴 Map p96, C3

Long-standing Taling Pling has moved into more sophisticated digs in this low-rise 'community mall'. Luckily the menu remains the same, and spans largely seafood- and vegetable-based Thai dishes, including a handful made with the eponymous tart vegetable. Great for an upscale-feeling Thai meal that doesn't skimp on flavour. (Baan Silom, Soi 19, Th Silom; mains 145-255B; ⏱11am-10pm; ❄ 🗐; Ⓢ Surasak exit 3)

Ngwanlee Lung Suan CHINESE-THAI $$

22 ✕ Map p96, G1

This staple of copious consumption is still going strong after all these decades. If you can locate the entrance, squeeze in with the postclubbing crowd and try some of those Chinese-style street dishes you never dare to order elsewhere, such as jàp chài (Chinese-style stewed vegies) or hŏy lai pàt nám prík pŏw (clams stir-fried with chilli sauce and Thai basil). (cnr Soi Lang Suan & Th Sarasin; mains 50-900B; ⏱7am-3am; 🗐; Ⓢ Ratchadamri exit 2)

Kalapapruek THAI $

23 ✕ Map p96, C3

This is the sort of restaurant where you're bound to encounter big-haired ladies and stiff silk suits – in Bangkok, tell-tale signs of a quality meal. The diverse menu spans regional Thai specialities from just about every region, daily specials and, occasionally, seasonal treats as well. (27 Th Pramuan; mains 80-150B; ⏱8am-6pm Mon-Sat, to 3pm Sun; ❄ 🗐; Ⓢ Surasak exit 3)

Somboon Seafood THAI $$$

24 ✕ Map p96, D2

Somboon is known for doing the best curry-powder crab in town. Soy-steamed sea bass (ฺblah grà·pohng nêung see·éw) is also a speciality and, like all good Thai seafood, should be enjoyed with an immense platter of kôw pàt ฺboo (fried rice with crab) and as many friends as you can pull together. (📞 0 2233 3104; www.somboonseafood.com; cnr Th Surawong

& Th Narathiwat Ratchanakharin; mains 120-900B; ⏱4-11.30pm; ❄🅿; 🅢Chong Nonsi exit 3)

Sushi Tsukiji

JAPANESE $$$

25 🍴 Map p96, E2

Th Thaniya is home to many hostess bars catering to visiting Japanese, so naturally, the quality of the street's Japanese restaurants is high. Specialising in raw fish, dinner at Tsukiji – named after Tokyo's famous seafood market – will leave a significant dent in the wallet, so come for lunch, when the restaurant serves several exceedingly good-value sushi sets for as little as 198B. (Th Thaniya; sushi per item 60-700B; ⏱10am-11pm; ❄🅿; 🅜Si Lom exit 2, 🅢Sala Daeng exit 1)

Muslim Restaurant

MUSLIM-THAI $

26 🍴 Map p96, B3

Plant yourself in any random wooden booth of this ancient eatery for a glimpse into what restaurants in Bangkok used to be like. The menu, much like the interior design, doesn't appear to have changed much in the restaurant's 70-year history, and the birianis, curries and samosas are still more Indian-influenced than Thai. (1354-6 Th Charoen Krung; mains 40-140B; ⏱6.30am-5.30pm; ⚓Tha Oriental)

Soi 10 Food Centres

THAI $

27 🍴 Map p96, D2

These two adjacent hangarlike buildings tucked behind Soi 10 are the main lunchtime fuelling stations for this area's office staff. Choices range from southern-style *kôw gaang* (point-and-choose curries ladled over rice) to virtually every form of Thai noodle. (Soi 10, Th Silom; mains 20-60B; ⏱8am-2pm Mon-Fri; 🅜Si Lom exit 2, 🅢Sala Daeng exit 1)

Drinking

Moon Bar

BAR

28 🍺 Map p96, G3

The Banyan Tree Hotel's Moon Bar kick-started the rooftop trend, and as Bangkok continues to grow at a mad pace, the view from 61 floors up only gets better. Arrive well before sunset and grab a coveted seat to the right of the bar for the most impressive views. Save your shorts and/or sandals for another bar. (www.banyantree.com; 61st fl, Banyan Tree Hotel, 21/100 Th Sathon Tai; ⏱5pm-1am; 🅜Lumphini exit 2)

Tapas Room

NIGHTCLUB

29 🍺 Map p96, E2

Although it sits staunchly at the front of Bangkok's pinkest street, this long-standing two-level disco manages to bring in just about everybody. Come from Thursday to Saturday, when Tapas features a combination of DJs and live percussion. (114/17-18 Soi 4, Th Silom; admission 100B; ⏱9pm-2am; 🅜Si Lom exit 2, 🅢Sala Daeng exit 1)

Top Tip

Reservations

If you have a lot of friends in tow or will be attending a formal restaurant (including hotel restaurants), reservations are recommended. Bookings are also recommended for Sunday brunches and dinner cruises. Otherwise, you generally won't have a problem scoring a table at the vast majority of restaurants in Bangkok.

viva aviv

BAR

30 Map p96, A2

An enviable riverside location, casual open-air seating and a funky atmosphere make this new restaurant-ish bar a contender for Bangkok's best sunset-cocktail destination. Expect a pun-heavy menu (sample item: I 'foc'cat cia' name!) of pizzas, meaty snacks and salads that really is no joke. (www.vivaaviv.com; ground fl, River City, 23 Th Yotha; 11am-midnight; Tha Si Phraya or shopping centre shuttle boat from Tha Sathon (Central Pier))

Sirocco Sky Bar

BAR

31 Map p96, B3

Allegedly one of the highest alfresco bars in the world, Sky Bar, located on the 63rd floor of this upmarket restaurant compound, provides heart-stopping views over Mae Nam Chao Phraya. Note that the dress code doesn't allow access to those wearing shorts or sandals. (www.lebua.com/en/ the-dome-dining/sky-bar-bangkok; 63rd fl, Dome at State Tower, 1055 Th Silom; 6pm-1am; Saphan Taksin exit 3)

Wong's Place

BAR

32 Map p96, H3

Want to emulate the life of an in-the-know expat on a big night out? It's as easy as heading to Wong's, a legendarily divey drinking spot with an old-school soundtrack. Don't arrive before midnight, and we wish you luck in departing before the sun rises. (27/3 Soi Si Bamphen; 9pm-late Tue-Sun; Lumphini exit 1)

70's Bar

BAR

33 Map p96, G1

A tad too small to be a club proper, this retro-themed bar spins all the hits for Gen Y in the ultimate Me city. Like much of the strip it's located on, the clientele is mixed, but often verges on the pink side of the fence. (231/16 Th Sarasin; 6pm-1am; Ratchadamri exit 2)

Barley

BAR

34 Map p96, D2

The seemingly incongruous combo of Belgian beer and Thai-influenced snacks somehow works at this new bar. Seating is on the breezy rooftop or inside, occasionally in the company of live bands. Barley is located in the Food Channel building, between Soi 5 and Soi 7. (www.barleybistro.com; Food Channel, Th Silom; 8pm-late; Si Lom exit 2, Sala Daeng exit 2)

Entertainment

Lumphini Boxing Stadium

THAI BOXING

35 ⭐ Map p96, H3

The big-time *moo·ay tai* (Thai boxing, also spelt *muay thai*) fighters spar at Lumphini's coveted ring. Matches occur on Tuesday and Friday at 6.30pm and Saturday at 5pm. The stadium doesn't usually fill up until the main event, around 8pm. (Th Phra Ram IV; tickets 3rd/2nd class/ringside 1000/1500/2000B; Ⓜ Lumphini exit 3)

Bamboo Bar

LIVE MUSIC

36 ⭐ Map p96, A3

The Oriental's Bamboo Bar is famous for its live lounge jazz, which holds court inside a colonial-era cabin of lazy fans, broad-leafed palms and rattan decor. Contact ahead of time to see what artists are in residence during your visit. (📞 0 2236 0400; www .mandarinoriental.com/bangkok/fine-dining/the-bamboo-bar; Mandarin Oriental, 48 Soi 40, Th Charoen Krung; ⏱ 11am-1am Sun-Thu, to 2am Fri & Sat; 🚢 Tha Oriental or hotel shuttle boat from Tha Sathon (Central Pier))

Sala Rim Naam

DINNER THEATRE

37 ⭐ Map p96, A3

The historic Mandarin Oriental hosts a dinner theatre in a sumptuous Thai pavilion located across the river in Thonburi. The price is well above average, reflecting the means of the hotel's client base, and the perform-ance gets positive reviews. (📞 0 2437 3080; www.mandarinoriental.com/bangkok/fine-dining/sala-rim-naam; ground fl, Mandarin Oriental, Soi 40, Th Charoen Krung; tickets 2000B; ⏱ dinner & show 8.15-9.30pm; 🚢 Tha Oriental or hotel shuttle boat from Tha Sathon (Central Pier))

Patpong

RED-LIGHT DISTRICT

38 ⭐ Map p96, E2

One of the most famous red-light districts in the world. Today any 'charm' that the area once possessed has been eroded by modern tourism, and fake Rolexes and Diesel T-shirts are more ubiquitous than flesh. There is, of course, a considerable amount of

Patpong area

naughtiness going on, although much of it takes place upstairs and behind closed doors. (Soi Patpong 1 & 2, Th Silom; ☉4pm-2am; M Si Lom exit 2, S Sala Daeng exit 1)

Shopping

House of Chao   ANTIQUES

39 🔒 | Map p96, D2

This three-storey antiques shop, appropriately located in an antique house, has everything that's necessary for you to deck out your fantasy colonial-era mansion. Particularly interesting are the various weather-worn doors, doorways, gateways and trellises that can be found in the covered area behind the showroom. (9/1 Th Decho, Silom; ☉9.30am-7pm; S Chong Nonsi exit 3)

River City   ANTIQUES

40 🔒 | Map p96, A2

Only got time for one antique shop? This four-storey complex of art and antiques is a one-stop shop for a Burmese Buddha image, black silk or a *benjarong* (traditional royal Thai ceramics) tea set, and you pay for the quality. The stores can arrange to ship your buys back home. (www.rivercity.co.th; 23 Th Yotha; ☉10am-10pm, many shops close Sun; S Saphan Taksin exit 2 & shopping centre shuttle boat from Tha Sathon (Central Pier), Tha Si Phraya)

Jim Thompson   TEXTILES

41 🔒 | Map p96, E2

This Jim Thompson is the largest shop of the business founded by the international promoter of Thai silk. It sells colourful silk handkerchiefs, placemats, wraps and cushions. The styles and motifs appeal to older,

---

Understand

7-Eleven Forever

Be extremely wary of any appointment that involves the words 'meet me at 7-Eleven'. In Bangkok alone, there are 2700 branches of 7-Eleven (known as *sair·wên* in Thai) – nearly a third the number found in all of North America. In central Bangkok, 7-Elevens are so ubiquitous that it's not uncommon to see two branches staring at each other from across the street. Although the company reports that its stores carry more than 2000 items, the fresh flavours of Thai cuisine are not reflected in the wares of a typical Bangkok 7-Eleven, the food selections of which are even junkier than those of its counterparts in the West. As in all shops in Thailand, alcohol is only available from 11am to 2pm and 5pm to midnight, and branches of 7-Eleven located near hospitals, temples and schools do not sell alcohol or cigarettes at all.

Understand

Patpong

Super Pussy! Pussy Collection! The neon signs leave little doubt about the dominant industry in Patpong, the world's most infamous strip of go-go bars. There is enough skin on show in Patpong to make Hugh Hefner blush, and a trip to an upstairs club could mean you'll never look at a ping-pong ball or a dart the same way again.

Roots in 'R&R'

Patpong occupies two soi that run between Th Silom and Th Surawong in Bangkok's financial district. The streets are privately owned by – and named for – the Chinese-Thai Patpongpanich family, who bought the land in the 1940s and built Patpong Soi 1 and its shophouses; Soi 2 was laid later. During the Vietnam War the first bars and clubs opened to cater to American soldiers on 'R&R'. The scene grew through the '70s and peaked in the '80s, when official Thai tourism campaigns made the sort of 'sights' available in Patpong a pillar of their marketing.

Prostitution in Thailand

Prostitution is illegal in Thailand but there are as many as two million sex workers, the vast majority of whom – women and men – cater to Thai men. Many come from poorer regional areas, such as Isan in the northeast, while others might be students helping themselves through university. Sociologists suggest Thais often view sex through a less moralistic filter than Westerners. That doesn't mean Thai wives like their husbands using prostitutes, but it's only recently that the empowerment of women through education and employment has led to a more vigorous questioning of this very widespread practice.

Patpong Today

Patpong has mellowed. Thanks in part to the popular night market that fills the soi after 5pm, it draws so many tourists that it has become a sort of sex theme park. There are still plenty of the stereotypical middle-aged men ogling pole dancers, sitting in dark corners of the so-called 'blow-job bars' and paying 'bar fines' to take girls to hotels that charge by the hour. But you'll also be among other tourists and families who come to see what all the fuss is about.

somewhat more conservative tastes. There's also a factory outlet just up the road, which sells discontinued patterns at a significant discount. (www .jimthompson.com; 9 Th Surawong; ⏱9am-9pm; Ⓜ Si Lom exit 2, Ⓢ Sala Daeng exit 3)

Old Maps & Prints ANTIQUES

42 🔒 Map p96, A2

You could poke around in this shop for hours, flipping through the maps of Siam and Indochina, laughing at early explorers' quaint drawings of 'the natives' and sighing with delight at the exquisite framed prints. (4th fl, River City, Th Yotha; ⏱11am-6pm Mon-Sat, 1-6pm Sat & Sun; Ⓢ Saphan Taksin exit 2 & shopping centre shuttle from Tha Sathon (Central Pier), Tha Si Phraya)

Tamnan Mingmuang HANDICRAFTS

43 🔒 Map p96, F2

As soon as you step through the doors of this museumlike shop, the earthy smell of dried grass and stained wood rushes to meet you. Rattan, *yahn li·pow* (a fernlike vine), water hyacinth woven into silklike patterns, and coconut shells carved into delicate

Top Tip

Counterfeits

Bangkok is ground zero for the production and sale of counterfeit goods. Although the price may be enticing, keep in mind that counterfeit goods are almost always as shoddy as they are cheap.

bowls are among the exquisite pieces that will outlast flashier souvenirs available on the streets. (2nd fl, Thaniya Plaza, Soi Thaniya; ⏱11am-8pm; Ⓜ Si Lom exit 2, Ⓢ Sala Daeng exit 1)

Lin & Sons Jewellers JEWELLERY

44 🔒 Map p96, B3

Lin might be a bit pricier than your average Bangkok silver shop, but you know you're getting the genuine article. Available are classic pieces like silver chokers, thick bangles and custom-engraved cuff links. (14 Soi 40, Th Charoen Krung; ⏱9am-6.30pm Mon-Sat; 🚤Tha Oriental)

Maison Des Arts HANDICRAFTS

45 🔒 Map p96, B3

Hand-hammered, stainless-steel tableware haphazardly occupies this warehouse retail shop. The bold style of the flatware dates back centuries and staff apply no pressure to indecisive shoppers. (1334 Th Charoen Krung; ⏱11am-6pm Mon-Sat; 🚤Tha Oriental)

Thai Home Industries HANDICRAFTS

46 🔒 Map p96, A3

Not your average Bangkok souvenir shop; a visit to this enormous traditional Thai building is a lot like picking around an abandoned attic of traditional Thai booty. The staff leave you to your own devices to poke around the bronzeware, silverware (especially cutlery) and basketry. (35

Moon Bar (p105)

Soi 40, Th Charoen Krung; ⏰9am-6.30pm
Mon-Sat; 🚢Tha Oriental)

Patpong Night Market MARKET

47 🔒 Map p96, E2

You'll be faced with the competing
distractions of strip-clubbing and
shopping on this infamous street.
And true to the area's illicit leanings,
pirated goods (in particular watches)
make a prominent appearance even
amid a wholesome crowd of families
and straight-laced couples. Bargain
with determination, as first-quoted
prices tend to be astronomically high.
(Soi Patpong 1 & 2, Th Silom; ⏰6pm-midnight;
Ⓜ Si Lom exit 2, Ⓢ Sala Daeng exit 1)

Chiang Heng HOUSEWARES

48 🔒 Map p96, A4

In need of a handmade stainless-
steel wok, old-school enamel-coated
crockery or a manually operated
coconut-milk strainer? Then we suggest you stop by this third-generation
family-run kitchen-supply store. Even
if your cabinets are already stocked,
a visit here is a glance into the type
of specialised and cramped but
atmospheric shops that have all but
disappeared from Bangkok. (1466 Th
Charoen Krung; ⏰10.30am-7pm; Ⓢ Saphan
Taksin exit 3)

Local Life
RCA

Getting There

Ⓜ **MRT** Phra Ram 9 exit 3 and taxi

The strip of dance clubs, live-music clubs and bars known as RCA (Royal City Avenue) has long been the first nightlife destination of choice for many young locals. In recent years, the clientele has grown up, and RCA now hosts locals and visitors of just about any age and has an increasingly sophisticated spread of bars and nightclubs to match.

1 Slim/Flix

Ideal for the indecisive raver, **Slim/ Flix** (29/22-32 Royal City Ave, off Th Phra Ram IX; ⏰9pm-2am; Ⓜ Phra Ram 9 exit 3 & taxi) is a huge complex dominating the north end of RCA. There's chilled house on one side (Flix), while the other (Slim) does the hip-hop/R&B soundtrack found across much of the city. Packed on weekends.

2 Route 66

Route 66 (www.route66club.com; 29/33-48 Royal City Ave, off Th Phra Ram IX; ⏰8pm-2am; Ⓜ Phra Ram 9 exit 3 & taxi) has been around almost as long as RCA. Top 40 hip hop rules the main space, but other 'levels' feature everything from Thai pop to live music.

3 Patisserie Mori Osaka

The Japanese pedigree may confuse some, but **Patisserie Mori Osaka** (www .facebook.com/patisseriemoriosaka; Block C, RCA, off Th Phra Ram IX; pastry 90-130B; ⏰11am-10pm; Ⓜ Phra Ram 9 exit 3 & taxi) actually does some of the better Western-style pastries in Bangkok.

4 Castro

Castro (www.facebook.com/Castro.rca .bangkok; Block C, RCA, off Th Phra Ram IX; ⏰10pm-5am; Ⓜ Phra Ram 9 exit 3 & taxi) is a booming gay club that seems to host a never-ending stream of pageants and contests. Open late.

5 LED

The size of a warehouse, **LED** (www .facebook.com/LEDclub; Block C, RCA, off Th Phra Ram IX; ⏰9.30pm-2am Tue-Sun; Ⓜ Phra Ram 9 exit 3 & taxi) pulls in the big-name DJs from around the globe. Outside the big events, it can be virtually empty – or even closed. Check the Facebook page.

6 Cosmic Café

Lower key than most places on RCA, **Cosmic** (Block C, RCA, off Th Phra Ram IX; ⏰8pm-2am Mon-Sat; Ⓜ Phra Ram 9 exit 3 & taxi) calls itself a cafe but looks like a bar, and has recently become one of Bangkok's better live-music clubs.

7 Taksura

Yet another chilled RCA destination, **Taksura** (RCA, off Th Phra Ram IX; ⏰6pm-2am; Ⓜ Phra Ram 9 exit 3 & taxi) is an open-air live-music pub with a retro theme. If you've got food on your mind, Taksura's spicy/tart *gàp glâam* (Thai drinking snacks) won't disappoint.

8 Zeta

Bangkok's only lesbian dance club at the time of writing, **Zeta** (29/67-69 RCA, off Phra Ram IX; ⏰10pm-2am; Ⓜ Phra Ram 9 exit 3 & taxi) is a huge disco with a nightly band (Mister Sister) doing Thai and Western covers. Only women are allowed entry. Packed on weekends.

9 House

House (www.houserama.com; 3rd fl, RCA Plaza, RCA, off Th Phra Ram IX; Ⓜ Phra Ram 9 exit 3 & taxi) is Bangkok's first and only art-house cinema, and shows lots of non-Hollywood foreign flicks.

Explore

Thanon Sukhumvit

Japanese enclaves, French restaurants, Middle Eastern nightlife zones, tacky 'sex-pat' haunts: it's all here along Th Sukhumvit, Bangkok's unofficial international zone. Where temples and suburban rice fields used to be, today you'll find shopping centres, nightlife and a host of other tidy amenities that cater to middle-class Thais and resident foreigners.

The Sights in a Day

☀ Begin your day with a swing through **Khlong Toey Market** (p118), central Bangkok's largest and most hectic market. Afterward, ride the MRT to the significantly more sedate Thai house museum, **Ban Kamthieng** (p118).

☀ Take advantage of Th Sukhumvit's spread of international cuisines and have a Middle Eastern lunch at **Nasir Al-Masri** (p120). Get fitted for a suit at one of the nearby tailors, such as **Raja's Fashions** (p128). Wind down with a Thai-style massage at **Coran** (p118) or **Asia Herb Association** (p118).

🌙 Kick the evening off with cocktails and art at **WTF** (p123). For dinner, consider upscale Thai at **Bo.lan** (p118) or Korean barbecue at **Myeong Ga** (p120). Continue with live music at **Living Room** (p126) or **Titanium** (p126), followed by dancing at **Bed Supperclub** (p123) or a Soi Ekamai club such as **Arena 10** (p123).

💜 **Best of Bangkok**

Foreign Cuisine Dining
Boon Tong Kiat Singapore Hainanese Chicken Rice (p120)

Nasir Al-Masri (p120)

Myeong Ga (p120)

Dance Clubs
Bed Supperclub (p123)

Arena 10 (p123)

Quirky Souvenirs
ThaiCraft Fair (p127)

ZudRangMa Records (p128)

Thai Massage
Asia Herb Association (p118)

Coran (p118)

Live Music
Titanium (p126)

Museums
Ban Kamthieng (p118)

Getting There

🅂 Nana, Asok, Phrom Phong, Thong Lo and Ekkamai

Ⓜ Khlong Toei, Queen Sirikit National Convention Centre, Sukhumvit and Phetchaburi

⚓ **klorng boat** Tha Asoke and Tha Nana Chard

Khlong Saen Saeb

For reviews see
- Sights p118
- Eating p118
- Drinking p123
- Entertainment p126
- Shopping p127

0   500 m
0   0.25 miles

Soi 39

Soi Phrom Si 2

Soi Prom Si 1

Soi Ekamai 21   18

40
Soi 49/9

Soi Thong Lor 16

Soi Thong Lor 13

Soi Thong Lor 15

6

Soi Prommit

Soi 49

22
31

Soi 39

20

Soi 63 (Ekamai)

Soi Ekamai 5

14

Soi Ekamai 10

32

Soi 45

Soi 49

Soi 51

Soi Thong Lor 5

Soi 55 (Thong Lor)

Th Sukhumvit

Soi Thong Lor 1

37
16

Soi 53

Soi Ekamai 6

Soi Ekamai 4

5

Thong Lo
15

Soi 36

Soi 38

Soi Ekamai 2

Eastern Bus
Terminal

Ekkamai

Sights

Ban Kamthieng
MUSEUM

1 ⊙ Map p116, C2

Ban Kamthieng is a merging of pretty architecture with museum learning. Built in the Lanna style, this 1844 house shows how a northern Thai family lived, complete with thorough explanations of Lanna beliefs, rituals and ceremonies. (บ้านคำเที่ยง; Siam Society, 131 Soi 21 (Asoke), Th Sukhumvit; adult/child 100B/free; ⊙9am-5pm Tue-Sat; Ⓜ Sukhumvit exit 1, Ⓢ Asok exit 3 or 6)

Khlong Toey Market
MARKET

2 ⊙ Map p116, B5

This wholesale market, one of the city's largest, is inevitably the origin of many of the meals you'll eat during your stay in Bangkok. Although some corners of the market can't exactly be described as photogenic, you'll want to bring a camera to capture the cheery fishmongers and photogenic stacks of fruit. Get there early – ideally before 9am. (ตลาดคลองเตย; cnr Th Ratchadaphisek & Th Phra Ram IV; ⊙5-10am; Ⓜ Khlong Toei exit 1)

Eating

Bo.lan
THAI $$$

3 ✖ Map p116, D4

Bo and Dylan (Bo.lan, a play on words that also means 'ancient'), former chefs at London's Michelin-starred nahm, have provided Bangkok with a compelling reason to reconsider upscale Thai cuisine. The couple's scholarly approach to cooking takes the form of seasonal set meals with

---

Ⓠ Local Life

Spa Central

Th Sukhumvit is home to many of Bangkok's recommended and reputable massage studios, including the following:

▶ **Asia Herb Association** (Map p116, F4; 📞 0 2392 3631; www.asiaherbassociation .com; 58/19-25 Soi 55 (Thong Lor), Th Sukhumvit; ⊙9am-midnight; Ⓢ Thong Lo exit 3) This chain specialises in massage using *brà·kóp*, compresses filled with 18 herbs.

▶ **Coran** (Map p116, B1; 📞 0 2651 1588; www.coranbangkok.com; 27/1-2 Soi 13, Th Sukhumvit; Thai massage per hr 400B; ⊙11am-10pm; Ⓢ Nana exit 3) A classy, low-key spa housed in a Thai villa.

▶ **Divana Massage & Spa** (Map p116, C2; 📞 0 2261 6784; www.divanaspa.com; 7 Soi 25, Th Sukhumvit; spa treatments from 2350B; ⊙11am-9pm Mon-Fri, 10am-9pm Sat & Sun; Ⓜ Sukhumvit exit 2, Ⓢ Asok exit 6) Divana retains a unique Thai touch with a private setting in a garden house.

VIVIANE PONTI/GETTY IMAGES ©

Tailor, Th Sukhumvit

antiquated dishes you're not likely to find elsewhere. (📞 0 2260 2962; www .bolan.co.th; 42 Soi Rongnarong Phichai Song-khram, Soi 26, Th Sukhumvit; set meal 1880B; ⏰ 6pm-midnight Tue-Sun; ❄️ 📱; Ⓢ Phrom Phong exit 4)

Quince INTERNATIONAL $$

4 🍴 Map p116, E4

This new kid on the block has made an audible splash on Bangkok's dining scene with its unique retro-industrial ambience and an Aussie-feeling, internationally influenced menu. Think meaty, seemingly deli-derived dishes such as wet roasted chicken, saffron and almond broth, barley and harissa. Reservations recommended. (📞 02 662 4478; www.quincebangkok.com; Soi 45, Th Sukhumvit; mains 200-1800B; ⏰ 11.30am-1am; ❄️ 🖋️ 📱; Ⓢ Phrom Phong exit 3)

Soul Food Mahanakorn THAI $$

5 🍴 Map p116, F4

In less than a year, and despite being run by a *fa·ràng* (foreigner) from Pennsylvania, Soul Food has shot to the top of the heap of cool places to eat Thai food in Bangkok. The secret recipe? We reckon it's Soul Food's dual nature as both an inviting restaurant and a bar serving boozy, Thai-influenced cocktails. (📞 0 2714 7708; www.soulfoodmahanakorn.com; 56/10 Soi 55 (Thong Lor), Th Sukhumvit; mains 180-275B; ⏰ 5.30pm-midnight; ❄️ 🖋️ 📱; Ⓢ Thong Lo exit 3)

Top Tip

Tipping

You shouldn't be surprised to learn that tipping in Thailand isn't as exact as it is in Europe (tip no one) or the USA (tip everyone). Thailand falls somewhere in between, and some areas are left open to interpretation. Some people leave roughly 10% at any sit-down restaurant where someone fills their glass every time they take a sip. Others don't. Most upmarket restaurants will apply a 10% service charge to the bill. Some patrons leave extra on top of the service charge; others don't. The choice is yours.

Boon Tong Kiat Singapore Hainanese Chicken Rice
SINGAPOREAN $

After taking in the exceedingly detailed and ambitious chicken rice manifesto written on the walls, order a plate of the restaurant's namesake and witness how a dish can be so simple, yet so delicious. And while you're there, you'd be daft not to order *rojak*, the spicy/sour fruit 'salad', which is cheekily referred to here as 'Singapore Som Tam'. (440/5 Soi 55 (Thong Lor), Th Sukhumvit; mains 60-150B; ⏲lunch & dinner; ❄ 🔊; ⑤Thong Lo exit 3 & taxi)

Nasir Al-Masri
EGYPTIAN $$

7 🍴 Map p116, A1

Part restaurant, part shrine to the glories of stainless-steel furnishings, this popular Egyptian joint simply can't be missed. This is Muslim food, with the emphasis on meat, but the kitchen also pulls off some brilliant veggie meze as well. Aid your postprandial digestion with a puff on the hookah

in the streetside patio area. (4/6 Soi 3/1, Th Sukhumvit; mains 160-370B; ⏲24hr; ❄ 🔊 🔊; ⑤Nana exit 1)

Myeong Ga
KOREAN $$

8 🍴 Map p116, B2

Located on the ground floor of Sukhumvit Plaza (the multistorey complex also known as Korean Town), this restaurant is the city's best destination for authentic Seoul food. Go for the tasty prepared dishes or, if you've got a bit more time, the excellent, DIY Korean-style barbecue. (ground fl, Sukhumvit Plaza, cnr Soi 12 & Th Sukhumvit; mains 200-850B; ⏲11am-10pm Tue-Sun, 4-10pm Mon; ❄ 🔊; Ⓜ Sukhumvit exit 3, ⑤Asok exit 2)

Tenkaichi Yakiton Nagiya
JAPANESE $

9 🍴 Map p116, D5

Originating in Tokyo, this equal parts cosy and hectic eatery is one of Bangkok's best and most popular *izakayas*, or Japanese tavern-style restaurants. The highlights here are the warming *nabe* (do-it-yourself hotpots) and the smokey *yakitoshi* (grilled skewers of meat). Expect lots of Japanese-style welcoming – some might call it shouting – by the staff, and on weekends, a queue. (www.nagiya.com; Nihonmachi 105, 115 Soi 26, Th Sukhumvit; mains 90-160B; ⏰5pm-midnight; ❋🅿; 🅂Phrom Phong exit 4 & taxi)

Snapper SEAFOOD $$

10 🍴 Map p116, B1

Allegedly Bangkok's first restaurant serving New Zealand cuisine, Snapper specialises in Kiwi-style fish and chips. Choose one of four sustainably harvested fish from New Zealand, your cut of fries, and the delicious homemade tartar sauce or a garlic aioli. A handful of other seafood dishes and salads and a brief wine list round out the selections. (www.snapper-bangkok.com; 1/22 Soi 11, Th Sukhumvit; mains 180-590B; ⏰5pm-midnight; ❋🅿; 🅂Nana exit 3)

Firehouse AMERICAN $$

11 🍴 Map p116, B1

There's lots of juicy debate on the topic of Bangkok's best burger, but this new place gets our vote. If burgers aren't your thing, try one of the

Top Tip
Smoking
Smoking has been outlawed at all indoor (and some quasi-outdoor) entertainment places since 2008.

homey American dishes influenced by fire stations across the US. Open late, and strategically located near Soi 11's discos, it's the perfect post-club meal. (www.firehousethailand.com; Soi 11, Th Sukhumvit; mains 150-380B; ⏰11.30am-3am; ❋🅿; 🅂Nana exit 3)

Bei Otto GERMAN $$

12 🍴 Map p116, C3

Claiming a Bangkok residence for nearly 30 years, Bei Otto's major culinary bragging point is its pork knuckles, reputedly the best in town. A good selection of German beers and an attached delicatessen with brilliant breads and super sausages makes it even more attractive to go Deutsch. (www.beiotto.com; 1 Soi 20, Th Sukhumvit; mains 175-590B; ⏰11am-midnight; ❋🔧🅿; Ⓜ Sukhumvit exit 2, 🅂Asok exit 4)

Local Life
Sunday Brunch

Sunday brunch has become a Bangkok institution – particularly among the members of the city's expat community – and the hotels along Th Sukhumvit offer some of the best spreads.

▶ **Rang Mahal** (Map p116, C3; 📞 0 2261 7100; 26th fl, Rembrandt Hotel, 19 Soi 20, Th Sukhumvit; buffet 850B; ⏱ 11am-2.30pm Sun; Ⓜ Sukhumvit exit 2, Ⓢ Asok exit 6) One of the most popular destinations for Bangkok's South Asian expat community.

▶ **Sunday Jazzy Brunch** (Map p116, B2; 📞 0 2649 8888; 1st fl, Sheraton Grande Sukhumvit, 250 Th Sukhumvit; adult/child 2600/1200B; ⏱ noon-3pm Sun; Ⓜ Sukhumvit exit 3, Ⓢ Asok exit 2) The Sheraton's Sunday brunch unites all the hotel's restaurant outlets to a theme of live jazz.

▶ **Marriott Café** (Map p116, A1; 📞 0 2656 7700; ground fl, JW Marriott, 4 Soi 2, Th Sukhumvit; buffet 1884B; ⏱ 11.30am-3pm Sat & Sun; Ⓢ Nana exit 3) The weekend brunch at this American hotel chain is likened to Thanksgiving year-round.

Saras
INDIAN, VEGETARIAN $

13 🍴 Map p116, C3

Describing yourself as a 'fast-food feast' may not be the cleverest PR move we've ever encountered, but it's a spot-on description of this casual Indian restaurant. Order at the counter to be rewarded with crispy *dosai*, regional set meals, rich curries or other meat-free dishes (dishes are brought to your table). (www.saras .co.th; Soi 20, Th Sukhumvit; mains 90-255B; ⏱ 8.30am-10.30pm; ✳ 🍴 📱; Ⓜ Sukhumvit exit 2, Ⓢ Asok exit 4)

Supanniga Eating Room
THAI $$

14 🍴 Map p116, G3

Following the current trend of serving regional Thai food in an upscale setting, this attractive eatery does a menu of unique dishes, many culled from Thailand's western provinces. It's not all about image, though, and the obscure Thai-style dips, tart salads and rich curries deliver. (www.facebook .com/SupannigaEatingRoom; 160/11 Soi 55 (Thong Lor), Th Sukhumvit; mains 120-350B; ⏱ 11.30am-2.30pm & 5.30-11.30pm Tue-Sun; ✳ 📱; Ⓢ Thong Lo exit 3 & taxi)

Soi 38 Night Market
THAI $

15 🍴 Map p116, F5

After a hard night of clubbing on Th Sukhumvit, head to this small but beloved knot of open-air food vendors. If you're going sober, stick to the knot of 'famous' stalls tucked into an alley on the right-hand side as you enter the street. (cnr Soi 38 & Th Sukhumvit; mains 30-60B; ⏱ 8pm-3am; Ⓢ Thong Lo exit 4)

Drinking

WTF
BAR

16 | Map p116, F4

Wonderful Thai Friendship is a funky and friendly neighbourhood bar that also packs in a gallery space and a multipurpose event locale. Artsy locals and resident foreigners come for the old-school cocktails, live music and DJ events, poetry readings, art exhibitions and truly tasty bar snacks. And we, like them, give WTF our vote for Bangkok's best pub. (www.wtfbangkok .com; 7 Soi 51, Th Sukhumvit; ⏰6pm-1am Tue-Sun; Ⓢ Thong Lo exit 3)

Cheap Charlie's
BAR

17 | Map p116, B1

You're bound to have a mighty difficult time convincing your Thai friends to go to Th Sukhumvit only to sit at an outdoor wooden shack decorated with buffalo skulls and wagon wheels. Fittingly, Charlie's draws a staunchly foreign crowd that doesn't mind a bit of kitsch and sweat with its Singha. (Soi 11, Th Sukhumvit; ⏰4.30-11.45pm Mon-Sat; Ⓢ Nana exit 3)

Tuba
BAR

18 | Map p116, H2

Used-furniture shop by day, Italian restaurant-bar by night; oddly enough, this business formula is not entirely unheard of in Bangkok. Pull up a leatherette lounge and take the plunge and buy a whole bottle for

once. And don't miss the delicious chicken wings. (34 Room 11-12 A, Soi Ekamai 21, Soi 63 (Ekamai), Th Sukhumvit; ⏰6pm-2am; Ⓢ Ekkamai exit 1 & taxi)

Bed Supperclub
NIGHTCLUB

19 | Map p116, B1

Resembling an illuminated tube, Bed has basked in the Bangkok nightlife limelight for a decade now, but has yet to lose any of its futuristic charm. Arrive at a decent hour to squeeze in dinner, or if you've only got dancing on your mind, come on Tuesday for the hugely popular hip-hop night. Admission starts at 600B; bring ID. (www .bedsupperclub.com; 26 Soi 11, Th Sukhuvmit; ⏰7.30pm-2am; Ⓢ Nana exit 3)

Arena 10
NIGHTCLUB DISTRICT

20 | Map p116, G3

This open-air entertainment zone is the destination of choice for Bangkok's young and beautiful – for the moment at least. Demo combines blasting beats and a NYC warehouse

---

Local Life

Club Alley

The streets that extend from Th Sukhumvit are home to many of Bangkok's most popular clubs. Ravers of uni age tend to head to Soi 63 (Ekamai), while the pampered elite play at Soi 55 (Thong Lor), and expats and tourists tend to gravitate towards the clubs on Soi 11.

Top Tip

The Numbers Game

All odd-numbered soi branching off Th Sukhumvit head north, while even numbers run south. Unfortunately, they don't line up sequentially (eg Soi 11 lies directly opposite Soi 8; Soi 39 is opposite Soi 26). Also, some larger soi are better known by alternative names, such as Soi Nana (Soi 3), Soi Asoke (Soi 21), Soi Thong Lor (Soi 55) and Soi Ekamai (Soi 63).

vibe, while Funky Villa, with its outdoor seating and Top 40 soundtrack, is more chilled. (cnr Soi Ekamai 5 & Soi 63 (Ekamai), Th Sukhumvit; ⏰6pm-2am; Ⓢ Ekkamai exit 2 & taxi)

Bar 23 BAR

21 Map p116, C4

The foreign NGO crowd and indie Thai types flock to this warehouse-like bar on weekend evenings; cold Beerlao and a retro-rock soundtrack keep them there until the late hours. Bar 23 is located about 500m down Soi 16, which is accessible from Th Ratchadaphisek. (Soi 16, Th Sukhumvit; ⏰7pm-1am Tue-Sat; Ⓜ Sukhumvit exit 2, Ⓢ Asok exit 6)

Iron Fairies BAR

22 Map p116, G3

Imagine, if you can, an abandoned fairy factory in Paris c 1912, and you'll begin to get an idea of the vibe at this popular pub/wine bar. If you manage

to wrangle one of a handful of seats, you can test this place's claim of serving Bangkok's best burgers. There's live music after 9.30pm. (www.theiron fairies.com; Soi 55 (Thong Lor), Th Sukhumvit; ⏰5pm-midnight Mon-Sat; Ⓢ Thong Lo exit 3 & taxi)

Nest BAR

23 Map p116, B1

Perched eight floors above ground on the roof of Le Fenix Hotel, Nest is a chic maze of cleverly concealed sofas and inviting chaise longues. A DJ soundtrack and one of the more thoughtful pub-grub menus in town keep things down to earth. (www .thenestbangkok.com; 8th fl, Le Fenix Hotel, 33/33 Soi 11, Th Sukhumvit; ⏰5pm-2am; Ⓢ Nana exit 3)

Alchemist BAR

24 Map p116, B1

The Alchemist is a tiny bar with a big emphasis on cocktails. It claims to do Bangkok's best Old Fashioned, and we don't tend to disagree. It also does live music and comedy nights – check the website for details. (www.thealchemistbkk .com; 1/19 Soi 11, Th Sukhumvit; ⏰5pm-midnight Tue-Sun; Ⓢ Nana exit 3)

Oskar BAR

25 Map p116, B1

It touts itself as a bistro, but Oskar is more like a cocktail bar dressed like a club – with food. Likewise, the drinks and dishes run the gamut, but are satisfying and cost less than the chic

setting would suggest. (www.oskar-bistro
.com; 24 Soi 11, Th Sukhumvit; ☻6pm-2am;
S Nana exit 3)

Glow

NIGHTCLUB

26 🚇 Map p116, C2

This self-proclaimed 'boutique' club
starts things early in the evenings
as a lounge boasting an impressive
spectrum of vodkas. As the evening
progresses, enjoy the recently
upgraded sound system and tunes
ranging from hip hop (Friday) to
electronica (Saturday) and everything
in between. Admission starts at 300B.
(www.glowbkk.com; 96/415 Soi Prasanmit, Th

Sukhumvit; ☻7pm-2am; **M** Sukhumvit exit 2,
S Asok exit 3)

Narz

NIGHTCLUB

27 🚇 Map p116, C2

The former Narcissus has undergone
a nip and tuck and now consists of
three separate zones boasting an
equal variety of music. It's largely a
domestic scene, but the odd guest DJ
can pull a large, diverse crowd. Open
later than most; admission starts
at 500B. (www.narzclubbangkok.net; 112
Soi Prasanmit, Th Sukhumvit; ☻10pm-late;
M Sukhumvit exit 2, **S** Asok exit 3)

Bed Supperclub (p123)

Top Tip

Opening Hours

Since 2004, authorities have ordered most of Bangkok's bars and clubs to close by 1am. A complicated zoning system sees venues in designated 'entertainment areas', including RCA, Th Silom, and parts of Th Sukhumvit, open until 2am, but even these 'later' licences are subject to police whimsy.

Q Bar   NIGHTCLUB

28 Map p116, B1

In club years, Q Bar has already reached retirement age, but a recent renovation ensures that it still holds a place in Bangkok's club scene. Most nights, the dance floor is monopolised by working girls and their pot-bellied admirers, but theme nights and celebrity DJs bring in just about everybody else in town. (www.qbarbangkok.com; 34 Soi 11, Th Sukhumvit; admission from 700B; ⊙8pm-2am; ⑤Nana exit 3)

Entertainment

Titanium   LIVE MUSIC

29 ⭐ Map p116, C3

Many come to this cheesy 'ice bar' for the chill, the skimpily dressed working girls and the flavoured vodkas. But we come for Unicorn, the all-female house band, who rock every night from 9.30pm to 12.30am. (www.titanium

bangkok.com; 2/30 Soi 22, Th Sukhumvit; ⊙8pm-1am; ⑤Phrom Phong exit 6)

Living Room   LIVE MUSIC

30 ⭐ Map p116, B2

Don't let looks deceive you: every night this bland hotel lounge transforms into one of the city's best venues for live jazz. And true to the name, there's comfy, sofa-based seating, all of it within earshot of the music. Enquire ahead of time to see which sax master or hide-hitter is in town. (☎0 2649 8888; www.sheraton grandesukhumvit.com/en/thelivingroom; Level 1, Sheraton Grande Sukhumvit, 250 Th Sukhumvit; ⊙6pm-midnight; ⓜSukhumvit exit 3, ⑤Asok exit 2)

Fat Gut'z   LIVE MUSIC

31 ⭐ Map p116, G3

This closet-sized 'saloon' combines live music and, er, fish and chips. Despite (or perhaps thanks to?) the odd whiff of chip oil, the odd combo works. Live blues every night from 9pm to midnight. (www.fatgutz.com; 264 Soi 12, Soi 55 (Thong Lor), Th Sukhumvit; ⊙6pm-2am; ⑤Thong Lo exit 3)

Sonic   LIVE MUSIC

32 ⭐ Map p116, H4

Live music in Bangkok usually means cheesy cover bands, but this new venue is pulling in original local indie outfits, not to mention some of the city's best DJs. Check the Facebook page to see what's on. (www.facebook .com/SonicBangkok; 90 Soi 63 (Ekamai), Th

Sukhumvit; ⊘6pm-2am; **S**Ekkamai exit 4 & taxi)

Soi Cowboy
RED-LIGHT DISTRICT

33 ⭐ Map p116, C2

This single-lane strip of raunchy bars claims direct lineage to the post-Vietnam War R&R era. A real flesh trade functions amid the flashing neon. (btwn Soi 21 (Asoke) & Soi 23, Th Sukhumvit; ⊘6pm-2am; **M**Sukhumvit exit 2, **S**Asok exit 3)

Nana Entertainment Plaza
RED-LIGHT DISTRICT

34 ⭐ Map p116, A1

Nana is a three-storey go-go bar complex where the sexpats are separated from the gawking tourists. It's also home to a few *gà·teu·i* (also spelled

kàthoey; transgender person) bars. (Soi 4 (Nana Tai), Th Sukhumvit; ⊘6pm-2am; **S**Nana exit 2)

Shopping
Nandakwang
HANDICRAFTS

35 🔒 Map p116, C2

The Bangkok satellite of a Chiang Mai store, Nandakwang sells a colourful mix of cheery, chunky, hand-embroidered pillows, dolls, bags and other cloth products. (www.nandakwang.com; 108/2-3 Soi Prasanmit, Th Sukhumvit; ⊘9am-6.30pm Mon-Sat; **M**Sukhumvit exit 2, **S**Asok exit 3)

Thanon Sukhumvit Market
MARKET

36 🔒 Map p116, B2

Leaving on the first flight out tomorrow morning? Never fear about gifts for those back home; here the street vendors will find you, with handbags, soccer kits, black-felt 'art', sunglasses and jewellery, to name a few. There are also ample stacks of nudie DVDs, Chinese throwing stars, penis-shaped lighters and other questionable gifts for your teenage brother. (btwn Soi 3 & Soi 15, Th Sukhumvit; ⏱11am-11pm Tue-Sun; Ⓢ Nana exits 1 & 3)

ZudRangMa Records   MUSIC STORE

37 🔒 Map p116, F4

Located next door to the popular bar WTF, the headquarters of this retro/world label offers a chance to finally combine the university-era pastimes of record-browsing and drinking. Come to snicker at corny old Thai vinyl covers or invest in some of the label's highly regarded compilations of classic *mŏr lam* and *lôok tûng* (Thai-style country music). (www.zudrangmarecords.com; 7/1 Soi 51, Th

Sukhumvit; ⏱noon-10pm Tue-Sun; Ⓢ Thong Lo exit 1)

Terminal 21   SHOPPING CENTRE

38 🔒 Map p116, C2

Seemingly satisfying a Thai need for wacky objects to be photographed in front of, this new themed mall is worth a visit for the spectacle as much as the shopping. Start at the floor-level 'airport' and proceed upwards through 'Paris', 'Tokyo' and other famous cities. Cheesiness aside, it's great for cheap couture, and 'San Francisco' is home to an immense food court. (www.terminal21.co.th; cnr Th Sukhumvit & Soi 21 (Asoke), Th Sukhumvit; ⏱10am-10pm; Ⓜ Sukhumvit exit 3, Ⓢ Asok exit 3)

Ⓠ Local Life
Bangkok's Savile Row

The strip of Th Sukhumvit between BTS stops Nana and Asok is home to the bulk of Bangkok's tailors.

▶ **Raja's Fashions** (Map p116, B2; ☎0 2253 8379; www.rajasfashions.com; 160/1 Th Sukhumvit; ⏱10am-8pm Mon-Sat; Ⓢ Nana exit 4) With his photographic memory for names, Bobby will make you feel as important as the long list of VIPs he's fitted over his decades in the business.

▶ **Rajawongse** (Map p116, A1; www.dress-for-success.com; 130 Th Sukhumvit; ⏱10.30am-8pm Mon-Sat; Ⓢ Nana exit 2) Jesse and Victor's creations are particularly renowned among American visitors and residents.

▶ **Ricky's Fashion House** (Map p116, A1; ☎0 2254 6887; www.rickysfashionhouse.com; 73/5 Th Sukhumvit; ⏱11am-10pm Mon-Sat & 1-5.30pm Sun; Ⓢ Nana exit 1) Ricky gets positive reviews for his more casual styles of custom-made trousers and shirts.

Fruit seller, Th Sukhumvit

Almeta   TEXTILES

39 🔒 Map p116, C2

If the verdant colours of Thai silk evoke frumpy society matrons, then you're a candidate for Almeta's more muted earth tones, similar in hue to raw sugar or lotus blossoms. (www .almeta.com; 20/3 Soi 23, Th Sukhumvit; ⏰10am-6pm; Ⓜ Sukhumvit exit 2, Ⓢ Asoke exit 3)

Sop Moei Arts   HANDICRAFTS

40 🔒 Map p116, F2

The Bangkok showroom of this nonprofit organisation features the vibrant cloth creations and baskets of Karen weavers in Mae Hong Son, northern Thailand. Located near the end of Soi 49/9, in the large Racquet Club complex. (www.sopmoeiarts.com; Soi 49/9, Th Sukhumvit; ⏰9.30am-5pm Sun-Fri; Ⓢ Phrom Phong exit 3 & taxi)

Top Sights
Chatuchak Weekend Market

Getting There

Located 6km north of Siam Sq

S Mo Chit exits 1 and 3

M Chatuchak Park exits 1 and 2, and Kamphaeng Phet exits 1 and 2

Imagine all of Bangkok's markets fused together in a seemingly never-ending commerce-themed barrio. Add a little artistic flair, a sauna-like climate and bargaining crowds and you've got a rough sketch of Chatuchak (also spelled 'Jatujak' or nicknamed 'JJ'), allegedly one of the world's largest markets. Everything is sold here, from live snakes to *mŏr lam* (Thai folk music) CDs, but the deeper you go, the clearer it becomes that Chatuchak is less about shopping and more about a unique Bangkok experience.

Bag stall, Chatuchak Weekend Market

Don't Miss

Antiques, Handicrafts & Souvenirs

Section 1 is the place to go for antique Buddha statues, old LPs and other random antiques; several shops in Section 10 sell Burmese lacquerware. Arts and crafts, ranging from musical instruments to hill-tribe items, can be found in Sections 25 and 26. Section 7 is a virtual open-air contemporary art gallery.

Clothing & Accessories

Clothing dominates much of Chatuchak, starting in Section 8 and continuing through the even-numbered sections to 24. Sections 5 and 6 deal in used clothing for every Thai youth subculture, from punks to cowboys. For accessories, several shops in Sections 24 and 26 specialise in chunky silver jewellery and semiprecious uncut stones.

Eating

Lots of Thai-style eating and snacking will stave off Chatuchak rage (cranky behaviour brought on by dehydration or hunger), and numerous food stalls, generally selling snacks and drinks, set up shop along the streets and lanes that border the market. The majority of sit-down style restaurants can be found at the periphery of most sections. If you need air-con, you can cross over to **Toh-Plue** (Th Kamphaengphet 2; ⊙11am-8pm; ❄; Ⓜ️Kamphaeng Phet) to get all the Thai standards.

Housewares & Decor

The western edge of the market, particularly Sections 8 to 26, specialises in all manner of housewares, from cheap plastic buckets to expensive brass woks. This area is a particularly good place to stock up on inexpensive Thai

---

www.chatuchak.org

Th Phahonyothin

⊙9am-6pm Sat & Sun

Ⓜ️Chatuchak Park exit 1, Kamphaeng Phet exits 1 & 2, Ⓢ Mo Chit exit 1 & 3

☑ Top Tips

▶ Arrive at Chatuchak Weekend Market as early as possible, as the crowds are thinner and the temperatures are slightly lower.

▶ An information centre and several banks with ATMs and foreign-exchange booths are near the northern end of the market's Soi 1, Soi 2 and Soi 3.

✕ Take a Break

There are lots of places to eat in the market; two of our faves are **Foon Talop** (Section 26, Stall 319, Soi 8), a north-eastern Thai-style restaurant, and **Café Ice** (Section 7, Stall 267, Soi 3), for good *pàt tai* (fried noodles).

ceramics, ranging from celadon to the traditional rooster-themed bowls from northern Thailand.

Pets

Possibly the most fun you'll ever have window-shopping will be petting puppies and cuddling kittens in Sections 13 and 15. Soi 9 of the former features several shops that deal solely in clothing for pets.

Plants & Gardening

The interior perimeter of Sections 2 to 4 features a huge variety of potted plants, flowers, herbs and fruits, and the accessories needed to maintain them. Many of these shops are also open on weekday afternoons.

Drinking

As evening draws near, down a beer at **Viva's** (Section 26, Stall 149, Soi 6), a cafe-bar that features live music and stays open late, or cross Th Kamphaengphet 2 to the cosy whisky bars, which keep nocturnal hours.

Nearby: Talat Rot Fai

Set in a sprawling former rail yard, **Talat Rot Fai** (ตลาดรถ ไฟ; Th Kamphaengphet; ⊙6pm-midnight Sat & Sun; Ⓜ Kamphaeng Phet exit 1) is all about retro, with goods ranging from antique enamel platters to secondhand Vespas. With mobile snack vendors, VW van–based bars and even a few land-bound pubs, it's also much more than just a shopping destination.

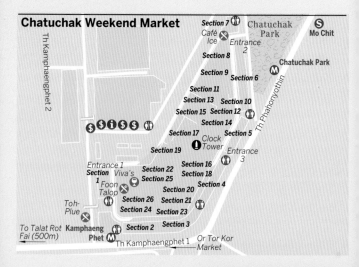

Understand
Bargaining

Many of your purchases at Chatuchak Weekend Market will involve an ancient skill that has long been abandoned in the West: bargaining. Contrary to what you may have seen elsewhere, bargaining is not a terse exchange of numbers and animosity. Rather, bargaining Thai style is a generally friendly transaction where two people try to agree on a price that is fair to both of them.

The first rule to bargaining is to have a general idea of the price. Ask around at a few vendors to get a rough notion. When you're ready to buy, it's generally a good strategy to start at 50% of the asking price. If you're buying several of an item, you have much more leverage to request a lower price. If the seller immediately agrees to your first price, you're probably paying too much, but it's bad form to bargain further at this point. Keeping a friendly, flexible demeanour throughout the transaction will almost always work in your favour.

Nearby: Or Tor Kor Market

Or Tor Kor (Th Kamphaengphet; ⏲8am-6pm; Ⓜ Kamphaeng Phet exit 3) is Bangkok's highest-quality fruit and agricultural market, and sights such as toddler-sized mangoes and dozens of pots full of curries amount to culinary trainspotting. Head to the market at lunchtime for its open-air food court, which features dishes from across Thailand. It's directly across Th Kamphaengphet from Chatuchak Weekend Market.

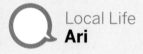

Local Life
Ari

Getting There

S Ari

Leafy Soi 7 off Th Phahonyothin, known colloquially as Ari, is an unassuming yet burgeoning
Bangkok hipster 'hood. There are no real sights
here, but the street and surrounding area are great
places to snack, eat and drink Thai-style. Start
your food tour with a sweet snack at Ka-nom or
iberry. Follow this with lunch: fried noodles at Phat
Thai Ari, a bowl of *khaw sawy*, or Thai veggie fare
at Baan Suan Pai. Let lunch settle then head to
Salt for some tunes and a pizza, before finishing
up with drinks and live music at Aree.

❶ Ka-nom

A self-proclaimed 'fashion bakery', **Ka-nom** (ground fl, La Villa, Th Phanonyothin; pastries 20-40B; ⏱10am-8pm; ❄; ⓢAriexIt 4) serves delicious *kà·nŏm kài*, baked sweets similar to Portuguese egg tarts, as well as coffee and other drinks.

❷ iberry

Iberry (www.iberryhomemade.com; ground fl, La Villa, Th Phahonyothin; ice cream from 35B; ⏱10.30am-8pm; ❄ 🍴; ⓢAriexit 4) is a domestic ice-cream chain serving unabashedly domestic flavours; think sorbets made from tart, refreshing gooseberry or tamarind, and ice creams laced with fragrant mango or rich Thai iced tea.

❸ Phat Thai Ari

Phat Thai Ari is one of Bangkok's better-known *pàt tai* shops. For something different, try the 'noodle-less' version, where strips of crispy green papaya are substituted for the traditional rice noodles. Phat Thai Ari is located on the unmarked lane that leads to Phaholyothin Center.

❹ Khao Soi Stall

Come lunchtime, this open-air **stall** (off Th Phahonyothin; mains from 30B; ⏱7am-2pm Mon-Fri; ⓢAriexit 3) serves deep bowls of *kâw soy*, a northern Thai curry noodle soup that's a rarity in Bangkok. Located in the unmarked alleyway adjacent to the bottom of BTS exit 3, it's sold from the stall farthest from Th Phahonyothin. No roman-script sign.

❺ Baan Suan Pai

The vegetarian equivalent of the mall food court, Baan Suan Pai is an open-air, wholesome-feeling gathering of vendors selling meat-free Thai-style dishes, drinks and desserts. It's located inside Banana Family Park, which is accessible from Th Phahonyothin or Soi Ari 1.

❻ Salt

With a DJ booth absent-mindedly flashing a copy of *Larousse Gastronomique*, **Salt** (cnr Soi Ari 4 (Nua) & Soi 7 (Ari), Th Phahonyothin; ⓢAriexit 3) is the kind of eclectic bar/restaurant that's shaping Bangkok's dining scene. The menu ranges from sushi to pizza, with an emphasis on grilled and smoked dishes.

❼ Aree

Exposed brick, chunky carpets and warm lighting give **Aree** (cnr Soi Ari 4 (Nua) & Soi 7 (Ari), Th Phahonyothin; ⏱6pm-1am; ⓢAriexit 3) a cosier feel than your average Bangkok bar. It also offers live music (from 8pm Tuesday to Sunday), contemporary Thai drinking snacks, and a drinks list with a few interesting single malts.

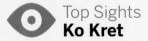

Top Sights
Ko Kret

Getting There

166 from Victory Monument to Pak Kret, before boarding the cross-river ferry (2B, 5am-9pm) from the pier at Wat Sanam Neua

Bangkok's easiest green getaway, Ko Kret is an artificial 'island', the result of a canal being dug nearly 300 years ago to shorten an oxbow bend in the Mae Nam Chao Phraya. The island is one of Thailand's oldest settlements of Mon people, who were a dominant tribe of central Thailand between the 6th and 10th centuries AD. Today, Ko Kret is known for its rural atmosphere, its distinctive pottery and its busy weekend market.

Terracotta pots, Ko Kret

Don't Miss

Wat Poramai Yikawat

Wat Poramai Yikawat (Ko Kret; admission free; ⊘9am-5pm), across from Ko Kret's main pier, has a Mon-style marble Buddha and a **museum** (Wat Poramai Yikawat, Ko Kret; admission free; ⊘1-4pm Mon-Fri, 9am-5pm Sat & Sun) with religious objects and exhibits on local pottery. But the temple's most famous landmark is undoubtedly the 200-year-old leaning stupa that juts out from the island's northeastern corner.

Pottery

Ko Kret is known for its hand-thrown terracotta pots, sold at markets throughout Bangkok; order an iced coffee from just about any vendor on the island and you'll get a small one as a souvenir. From Wat Poramai Yikawat, go in either direction to find both abandoned kilns and working pottery centres on the east and north coasts.

Touring the Island

A 6km paved path circles Ko Kret, and can be easily completed on foot or by bicycle, the latter available for rent from the pier (40B per day). Alternatively, it's possible to charter a boat for up to 10 people for 500B; the typical island tour stops at a batik workshop, a sweets factory and on weekends a floating market.

---

admission free

🚌166 & cross-river ferry from Wat Sanam Neua

☑ Top Tips

▶ Ko Kret can be horribly crowded on weekends; arrive on a weekday instead. There are fewer eating and shopping options, but you'll have the place to yourself.

✖ Take a Break

The northern coast of Ko Kret is home to a row of open-air restaurants, many serving *khâw châa*, an unusual but delicious Mon dish of savoury tit-bits served with chilled fragrant rice. **Pa Ka Lung** (Restaurant Rever Side; Ko Kret; mains 30-60B; ⊘8am-4pm Mon-Fri, to 6pm Sat & Sun; 🗐), an open-air food court with an English-language menu and sign, serves *khâw châa* and other Thai dishes.

The Best of
Bangkok

Bangkok's Best Walks

Bangkok's Best...

Bangkok by night
PETER ADAMS/GETTY IMAGES ©

Best Walks
Bangkok's Birthplace

🏃 The Walk

Most of Bangkok's 'must-see' destinations are found in the former royal district, Ko Ratanakosin. This walk takes in all of these, plus lower-key sights. It's best to start early to beat the heat and get in before the hordes descend. Dress modestly in order to gain entry to the temples, and ignore any strangers who approach you offering advice on sightseeing or shopping.

Start Tha Chang

Finish Wat Arun

Length 4km; three to four hours

✗ Take a Break

Ko Ratanakosin restaurants tend to be super-touristy or very street; for something in-between, try **Mangkud Cafe** (Club Arts; Map p34, B3; www .clubartsgallery.com; Soi Wat Rakhang; mains 125-300B; ⏰10.30am-11pm Tue-Thu, to midnight Fri-Sun; 🚤from Tha Chang).

Wat Pho (p28)

❶ Silpakorn University

Start at Tha Chang and follow Th Na Phra Lan east with a quick diversion to this institution, Thailand's premier fine-arts university.

❷ Wat Phra Kaew & Grand Palace

Continue east to the main gate into **Wat Phra Kaew & Grand Palace** (p24); these are two of Bangkok's most famous attractions.

❸ Trok Tha Wang

Return to Th Maha Rat and proceed north, through a gauntlet of herbal apothecaries and sidewalk amulet sellers. After passing the cat-laden newsstand (you'll know it when you smell it), turn left into Trok Tha Wang, a narrow alleyway holding a seemingly hidden classic Bangkok neighbourhood.

❹ Wat Mahathat

Returning to Th Maha Rat, continue moving north. On your right is Wat Mahathat, one of Thailand's most respected Buddhist universities.

5 Amulet Market

Across the street, turn left into crowded Trok Mahathat to see the cramped Amulet Market. As you continue north alongside the river, amulet vendors soon turn into food vendors.

6 Thammasat University

The emergence of white-and-black uniforms is a clue you're approaching Thammasat University, known for its law and political-science departments.

7 Sanam Luang

Exiting at Tha Phra Chan, cross Th Maha Rat and continue east until you reach Sanam Luang, the 'Royal Field'.

8 Lak Meuang

Cross the field and continue south along Th Ratchadamnoen Nai until you reach the home of Bangkok's city spirit, **Lak Meuang** (p36).

9 Wat Pho

Then head south along Th Sanam Chai and turn right onto Th Thai

Wang, which leads to the entrance of **Wat Pho** (p28), home of the giant reclining Buddha.

10 Wat Arun

If you've still got the energy, head to adjacent Tha Tien to catch the cross-river ferry to **Wat Arun** (p32), one of the few Buddhist temples you're encouraged to climb on.

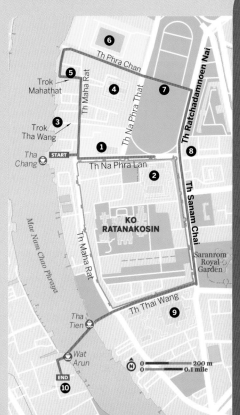

Best Walks
Riverside Architecture Ramble

🏃 The Walk

Bangkok isn't generally known for its architecture, but the road that runs along Mae Nam Chao Phraya, Th Charoen Krung (formerly known as New Road), is home to many of the city's noteworthy secular structures. In addition to unique architecture, the area was formerly the city's largest foreign enclave, and today continues to serve as a home to many of Bangkok's Muslim residents.

Start BTS Saphan Taksin

Finish viva aviv

Length 3km; two to four hours

🍴 Take a Break

To ensure that your meal complements the area's ethnic vibe, consider lunch or a snack break at **Muslim Restaurant** (Map p105, B3; 1354-6 Th Charoen Krung; mains 40-140B; ⏱6.30am-5.30pm; 🚤Tha Oriental), a time-warped eatery that dates back at least 70 years and serves tasty food.

Old Customs House

JOHN BORTHWICK/GETTY IMAGES ©

❶ Shophouses

Starting from the BTS stop at Saphan Taksin, walk north along Th Charoen Krung, passing the ancient shophouses between Th Charoen Wiang and Th Si Wiang.

❷ State Tower

At the corner with Th Silom is the imposing but ugly neoclassical State Tower. Pop up to the 63rd floor for a drink at **Sky Bar** (p106) in the evening.

❸ Mandarin Oriental

Turn left on Soi 40, home to the Mandarin Oriental, Bangkok's oldest and most storied hotel. The 1887 original structure remains today as the Author's Wing.

❹ East Asiatic Company

Across from the entrance of the Mandarin Oriental is the classical Venetian-style facade of the East Asiatic Company, built in 1901.

❺ Assumption Cathedral

Proceed beneath the overhead walkway

linking two buildings to the red-brick Assumption Cathedral, the current structure of which dates back to 1918.

❻ OP Plaza

Return to Soi 40 and take the first left. On your right is OP Plaza, today an antique mall, but originally built in 1905 as a department store.

❼ Old Customs House

Pass the walls of the French embassy and turn left. Head towards the river and the 1890s-era Old Customs House.

❽ Haroon Village

Backtrack and turn left beneath the green sign that says Haroon Mosque. You're now in Haroon Village, a Muslim enclave.

❾ General Post Office

Wind through Haroon and you'll eventually come to Soi 34, which leads back to Th Charoen Krung. Turn left and cross the street opposite the art deco General Post Office.

❿ Bangkokian Museum

Turn right onto Soi 43 and proceed to the **Bangkokian Museum** (p98), a compound featuring three antique wooden homes.

⓫ viva aviv

Continue along Captain Bush Lane to River City – not noteworthy in an architectural sense, but its riverside bar, **viva aviv** (p106), is a good place to end the walk.

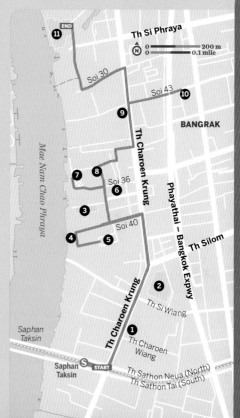

Best
Shopping

Prime your credit card and shine your baht, as shopping is serious business in Bangkok. Hardly a street corner in the city is free from a vendor, hawker or impromptu stall, and it doesn't stop there: Bangkok is also home to one of the world's largest outdoor markets, not to mention Southeast Asia's second-largest mall.

INGOLF POMPE/GETTY IMAGES ©

Malls & Markets

Although the tourist brochures tend to tout the upmarket malls, Bangkok still lags slightly behind Singapore and Hong Kong in this area, and the open-air markets are where the best deals and most original items are found.

Bargaining

At Bangkok's markets and at some of its malls, you'll have to bargain for most, if not all, items. In general, if you see a price tag, it means that the price is fixed and bargaining isn't an option.

Counterfeits

Bangkok is ground zero for the production and sale of counterfeit goods. Keep in mind that they're almost always as shoddy as they are cheap.

Gems & Jewellery

Countless tourists are sucked into a scam in which they're taken to a store by a helpful stranger and tricked into buying bulk gems that can supposedly be resold in their home country for 100% profit. The expert con artists seem trustworthy and convince tourists that they need a citizen of the country to circumvent tricky customs regulations. Unsurprisingly, the gem world doesn't work like that; what most tourists end up with are worthless pieces of glass.

☑ **Top Tips**

▶ **Nancy Chandler's Map of Bangkok**
(www.nancychandler.net) tracks all sorts of small, out-of-the-way shopping venues and markets, and dissects the innards of the Chatuchak Weekend Market.

Flower market

Best Markets

Chatuchak Weekend Market One of the world's largest markets and a must-do Bangkok experience. (p130)

Talat Rot Fai Retro-themed open-air market popular with Bangkok hipsters. (p132)

Th Khao San Market All the backpacker essentials. (p55)

Pak Khlong Talat Bangkok's famous nighttime flower market. (p65)

Talat Mai A slice of China in Bangkok. (p65)

Best for Quirky Souvenirs

ThaiCraft Fair Handicrafts made by community groups across Thailand. (p127)

ZudRangMa Records Pick up some vintage vinyl or an exotic compilation. (p128)

Nandakwang Uniquely colourful cloth housewares. (p127)

River City Unique antiques – if you've got the budget. (p108)

Best Malls

MBK Center A seemingly never-ending Thai market in a mall. (p86)

Siam Square A home away from home for Bangkok's budding fashionistas. (p87)

Siam Paragon Where Bangkok goes on Sunday. (p87)

Siam Center Tonnes of Thai labels. (p89)

Best
Museums

Bangkok's museums can't compete with those of Europe in terms of collection or sophistication, but the city is home to some truly unique institutions, ranging from an engaging insight into Siamese culture to a display on forensic science that's quite unlike anything else in the world.

JOHN BORTHWICK/GETTY IMAGES ©

Museum of Siam This fun and interactive museum offers a contemporary look at an ancient culture (p35)

Yaowarat Chinatown Heritage Center The low-down on Thai-Chinese culture. (p61)

Bangkokian Museum A house-bound museum that offers a peek into urban Bangkok life of yesteryear. (p98)

National Museum This expansive compound – itself a former minor palace – is Thailand's premier repository of national treasures. (p35)

Suan Pakkad Palace Museum This seemingly hidden walled compound is a fascinating depository of Thai art. (p91)

Royal Barges National Museum Home to what are arguably the world's most ostentatious canoes. (p36)

Songkran Niyomsane Forensic Medicine Museum & Parasite Museum As the name matter-of-factly indicates, this is hands-down Bangkok's most bizarre museum, and not a destination for the faint of heart. (p35)

☑ **Top Tips**

▶ Student discount cards are generally not recognised in Bangkok; thankfully admission to most institutions is relatively inexpensive.

▶ Many Bangkok museums are closed on Monday.

Ban Kamthieng Escape to rural northern Thailand – in the middle of modern Bangkok. (p118)

Best
Foreign Cuisine Dining

Contemporary Bangkok's menu extends far beyond Thai; reconsider rice for a meal and jump headfirst into a contemporary and sophisticated dining scene whose options range from Korean to French, touching on just about about everything in between.

MIKA CO. LTD./GETTY IMAGES ©

D'sens Contemporary fine dining with a southern French accent. (p102)

Boon Tong Kiat Singapore Hainanese Chicken Rice Where to sample Singapore's unofficial national dish. (p120)

Zanotti The place to go for pasta. (p103)

Nasir Al-Masri Authentic Egyptian in the heart of Bangkok's Middle Eastern 'hood. (p120)

Myeong Ga Seoul food in Bangkok's tiny Koreatown. (p120)

Shoshana A taste of Jerusalem in Bangkok. (p50)

Chennai Kitchen Bangkok's best destination for southern Indian cuisine. (p103)

Bei Otto It's Oktoberfest year round at this long-standing German restaurant. (p121)

Firehouse Where Americans go to eat when they're feeling homesick. (p121)

Tenkaichi Yakiton Nagiya An authentic Japanese drinking tavern. (p120)

☑ Top Tips

▶ Most upmarket restaurants will apply a 10% service charge to the bill. Some patrons leave extra on top of the service charge; others don't. The choice is yours.

▶ Keep up with the ever-changing international food scene in Bangkok by following the excellent restaurant reviews in **BK** (bk.asia-city.com/restaurants).

Best
Street Food

Nowhere is the Thai reverence for food more evident than in Bangkok. To the outsider, the life of a Bangkokian appears to be a string of meals and snacks punctuated by the odd stab at work, not the other way around. If you can adjust your mental clock to this schedule, your stay will be a delicious one indeed.

KYLIE MCLAUGHLIN/GETTY IMAGES ©

Street Stalls & Markets

Open-air markets and food stalls are among the most popular dining spots for Thais. In the mornings, stalls selling coffee and Chinese-style doughnuts spring up along busy commuter corridors. At lunchtime, diners might grab a plastic chair at yet another stall for a simple stir-fry. In Bangkok's suburbs, night markets often set up in the middle of town with a cluster of food vendors, metal tables and chairs.

Informal Restaurants

Lunchtime is the right time to point and eat at the typically open-air *ráhn kôw gaang* (rice and curry shops), which sell a selection of pre-made dishes. The more generic *ráhn ah·hǎhn đahm sàng* (made-to-order restaurant) can often be recognised by a display of raw ingredients and offers a standard repertoire of Thai and Chinese-Thai dishes.

Shophouse Restaurants

Arguably the most delicious type of eatery in Bangkok is the open-fronted shophouse restaurant. The cooks at these places have most likely been serving the same dish for several decades, and really know what they're doing. The food may cost slightly more than food sold from stalls, but the setting is usually more comfortable and hygienic.

☑ **Top Tips**

▶ Bangkok has passed a citywide ordinance banning street vendors from setting up shop on Mondays, so don't plan on having a street meal on this day.

▶ Written, photographed and maintained by the author of this book, www.austinbush photography. com/blog includes extensive coverage of streetside dining in Bangkok.

Street food vendor

Best Street Food

Thip Samai Bangkok's most legendary destination for *pàt tai*. (p50)

Nai Mong Hoi Thod Long-standing hole-in-the-wall serving delicious fried mussels. (p62)

Th Phadungdao Seafood Stalls These stalls are so street you risk getting bumped by a car. (p63)

Foon Talop Open-air dining in the middle of Chatuchak Weekend Market. (p131)

Pa Aew Ramshackle curry stall in old Bangkok. (p37)

Somtam Convent Shophouse restaurant serving northeastern Thai dishes. (p103)

Food Plus Narrow alleyway holding a string of curry vendors. (p82)

Gǒo·ay đěe·o kôo·a gài Fried noodles in a market alley. (p63)

Jék Pûi Curry stall famous for its lack of tables. (p63)

Mangkorn Khǒw Chinatown stall serving excellent wheat and egg noodles. (p63)

Best
Rooftop Bars

Bangkok is one of the few big cities in the world where nobody seems to mind if you slap the odd bar or restaurant on the top of a skyscraper. The options range from chic to cheap and, likewise, range in view from hyper-urban to suburban.

KAY MAERITZ/GETTY IMAGES ©

Moon Bar The combination of casual ambience and stunning views make this our personal fave of Bangkok's rooftop bars. (p105)

Sirocco Sky Bar The sweeping Hollywood entrance and seemingly floating bar mark this as the city's most sophisticated rooftop venue. (p106)

Sky Train Jazz Club Funky, seemingly hidden rooftop bar in a suburban 'hood. (p91)

Phra Nakorn Bar & Gallery Couple views over old Bangkok with some great bar snacks. (p52)

Nest Only nine floors above ground, this sleek rooftop bar makes up in style what is lacks in elevation. (p124)

Amorosa Elevated bar with one of Bangkok's best river views. (p39)

Red Sky Come to this chic rooftopper for a martini and an appropriately urban perspective on central Bangkok. (p85)

☑ **Top Tips**

▶ Dress accordingly; most of Bangkok's rooftop bars won't allow access to those wearing shorts or sandals.

▶ Forget about lighting up; smoking has been outlawed at all indoor and most outdoor bars and restaurants since 2008.

Best
Dance Clubs

Despite what your dodgy uncle told you, having a fun night out in Bangkok does not necessarily have to involve ping-pong balls or the word 'go-go'. As in any big international city, the nightlife scene in Bangkok ranges from classy to trashy, and touches on just about everything in between.

AUSTIN BUSH/GETTY IMAGES ©

Bangkok's Club Scene

Bangkok clubs burn strong and bright on certain nights – weekends, a visit from a foreign DJ or the music flavour of the month – then hibernate every other night. Hot spots cluster on the soi off Sukhumvit, Silom and RCA (Royal City Ave), the city's 'entertainment zones', which qualify for the 2am closing time.

Practicalities

Despite the relatively early closing time of 2am, most places don't begin filling up until midnight. Cover charges run as high as 700B and usually include a drink or two. You'll need ID to prove you're legal (20 years old); they'll card even the grey-haired.

☑ **Top Tips**

▶ To find out what's on, check out **Dude Sweet** (www.dudesweet.org), **Club Soma** (www.clubsoma.tumblr.com) or **Paradise Bangkok** (www.zudrangmarecords.com), all organisers of hugely popular monthly parties, or local listings rags such as *BK* or the *Bangkok Post's* Friday supplement, *Guru*.

Best Dance Clubs

Bed Supperclub Bangkok's top nightclub. (p123)

Tapas Room Tightly-packed, two-floor club with an unassuming vibe. (p105)

Arena 10 Where Bangkok's young and beautiful shake their young and beautifuls. (p123)

Club Dance with a virtual UN of partiers at this Th Khao San disco. (p43)

Route 66 Long-standing mega-club on the RCA nightlife strip. (p113)

Glow A boutique disco. (p125)

Narz Like dancing late? Come to this nocturnal complex. (p125)

Slim/Flix Another reason to make the trek out to RCA. (p113)

LED RCA club that pulls the occasional big-name DJ. (p113)

Q Bar A slightly cheesy Bangkok nightlife staple. (p126)

Best
Massage & Spa

Bangkok could mount a strong claim to being the massage capital of the world. According to the teachings of traditional Thai healing, the use of herbs and massage should be part of a regular health-and-beauty regimen, not just an excuse for pampering – music to the ears of many a visitor to Bangkok.

THOMAS PICKARD/GETTY IMAGES ©

Massage or Spa?

In Bangkok options run the gamut from storefront traditional Thai massage to an indulgent spa 'experience' with service and style. And even within the enormous spa category there are choices: there is still plenty of pampering going on, but some spas now focus more on the medical than the sensory, while plush resort-style spas offer a laundry list of hyper-specific treatments.

Thai Massage

Although traditional Thai massage (*nôo·at pǎan boh·rahn*) sounds relaxing, at times it can seem more closely related to Thai boxing than to shiatsu. Thai massage is based on yogic techniques for general health involving pulling, stretching, bending and manipulating pressure points. Full-body massages usually include camphor-scented balms or herbal compresses, or oil in cheaper establishments. A foot massage is arguably (and it's a strong argument) the best way to treat the legweariness of sightseeing.

Costs

Depending on the neighbourhood, massages in small parlours cost approximately 200B to 350B for an hour-long foot massage and 300B to 500B for an hour of full-body massage. Spa experiences start at about 800B and climb like a Bangkok skyscraper.

☑ **Top Tips**

▶ Be forewarned that 'oil massage' is sometimes taken as code for 'sexy massage'.

▶ Wat Pho Thai Traditional Medical and Massage School offers courses – taught in English – on Thai massage.

Massage treatment

Best Thai Massage

Health Land Great-value traditional Thai massage in a contemporary setting. (p99)

Asia Herb Association Massage with an emphasis on Thai-style herbal compresses. (p118)

Ruen-Nuad Massage Studio Charming house-bound massage studio. (p98)

Coran Tiny but classy massage studio. (p118)

Wat Pho Thai Traditional Medical and Massage School A massage studio in a temple. (p35)

Best Spas

Spa 1930 Cosy-feeling spa located in an antique house. (p79)

Thann Sanctuary Chic mall-bound spa employing fragrant herbal products. (p79)

Divana Massage & Spa Casual spa with a Thai vibe. (p118)

Best
For Kids

There aren't a whole lot of attractions in Bangkok meant to appeal directly to the little ones, but there's no lack of locals willing to provide attention. This means kids are welcome almost anywhere and you'll rarely experience the sort of eye-rolling annoyance often seen in the West.

Infants

Nappies (diapers), international brands of milk formula and other infant requirements are widely available. In general, Thai women don't breastfeed in public, though in department stores they'll often find a change room. For moving by foot, slings are often more useful than prams, as Bangkok footpaths are infamously uneven.

Eating with Kids

Dining with children in Thailand, particularly with infants, is a liberating experience, as Thai people are so fond of kids. Take it for granted that your kids will be fawned over, played with, and more often than not, carried around, by restaurant wait staff. It's worth noting that highchairs are rare apart from at expensive restaurants.

Best Kids Attractions

Lumphini Park Come here for kite flying (in season – February to April), boating and fish feeding. (p98)

Queen Saovabha Memorial Institute Antivenin-producing snake farm. (p99)

Siam Paragon In addition to an IMAX theatre, this mall also includes Siam Ocean World, a basement-level aquarium. (p87)

Siam Discovery Center Home to a branch of Madam Tussaud's. (p89)

LONELY PLANET/GETTY IMAGES ©

☑ Top Tips

▶ **Bambi** (www .bambiweb.org) is a useful resource for parents and kids in Bangkok.

▶ **Bangkok.com** (www.bangkok .com/kids) includes pages that have a dizzying array of things to do for kids.

Museum of Siam This museum has lots of interactive exhibits that will appeal to kids. (p35)

Best
Cooking Classes

Having consumed everything Bangkok has to offer is one thing, but imagine the points you'll rack up if you can make the same dishes for your friends back at home. A visit to a Thai cooking school has become a must-do for many Bangkok itineraries, and for some visitors it is a highlight of their trip.

LONELY PLANET/GETTY IMAGES ©

What to Expect

A typical half-day course should include a visit to a fresh market and/or an introduction to Thai ingredients and flavours, and a chance to prepare and cook three or four dishes. Nearly all lessons include a set of printed recipes and end with a communal lunch consisting of your handiwork.

Planning Ahead

Most Bangkok cooking schools offer dishes that change on a daily basis; check the websites to see what dishes are being taught during your visit. Arrange courses at least a couple of days in advance.

Best Cooking Classes

Helping Hands (☑08 4901 8717; www.cookingwith poo.com; 1200B; ◎lessons 8.30am-1pm) This popular cooking course was started by a native of Khlong Toey's slums and is held in her neighbourhood. Courses span four dishes and include a visit to Khlong Toey Market and transportation to and from Th Sukhumvit.

Baipai Thai Cooking School (☑0 2561 1404; www.baipai.com; 8/91 Soi 54, Th Ngam Wong Wan; lessons 2200B; ◎9.30am-1.30pm & 1.30-5.30pm Tue-Sat) Housed in an attractive suburban villa and taught by a small army of staff, Baipai offers two daily lessons of four dishes each. Transportation is available.

Blue Elephant Thai Cooking School (☑0 2673 9353; www.blueelephant .com; 233 Th Sathon Tai; lessons 2800B; ◎8.45am-1.15pm & 1.30-4.45pm Mon-Sat; S Surasak exit 2) This chi-chi school offers two lessons daily. The morning class squeezes in a visit to a local market; the afternoon session includes a detailed introduction to Thai ingredients.

Silom Thai Cooking School (☑08 4726 5669; www.bangkokthaicooking .com; 68 Soi 13, Th Silom; lessons 1000B; ◎lessons 9am-1pm, 1.40-5.30pm & 6-9pm; S Chong Nonsi exit 3). The facilities are basic but Silom crams a visit to a local market and instruction of six dishes into four hours, making it the best bang for your baht. Transportation is available.

Best
Temples

A Thai temple (wát) is a compound of different buildings serving specific religious functions. Even if you don't consider yourself spiritual, Bangkok's wát provide pleasures that range in scope from artistic inspiration to urban exploration.

EDUCATION IMAGES/UIG/GETTY IMAGES ©

Thai Architecture

Traditional Thai temple architecture follows strict rules of design that dictate proportion, placement, materials and ornamentation. In addition to the native Siamese styles of building, within Bangkok's temples you'll also find examples from historical Khmer, Mon, Lao and northern Thai traditions.

Buddha Images

Every wát in Bangkok has a Buddha image, usually sculpted according to strict iconographical rules found in Buddhist art texts dating to the 3rd century AD. There are four basic postures and positions: standing, sitting, walking and reclining.

Temple Murals

An astonishing variety of scenes from both secular and religious life embellish the inner walls of temples throughout Bangkok. Always instructional in intent, such painted images ranged from depictions of the *jatakas* (life stories of the Buddha) and scenes from the Indian Hindu epic Ramayana to elaborate scenes detailing daily life in Thailand.

Stupa

A classic component of temple architecture is one or more stupa (*chedi* in Thai), a solid mountain-shaped monument that pays tribute to the enduring stability of Buddhism. Many stupas are believed to contain 'relics' (pieces of bone) belonging to the Buddha.

☑ **Top Tips**

▶ At many of Bangkok's temples dress rules are strictly enforced, and if you're wearing shorts or a sleeveless shirt, you will not be allowed into the temple grounds – this applies to men and women.

▶ Shoes must be removed before entering any enclosed structure in a Thai wát.

Wat Suthat (p46)

Best Temples

Wat Phra Kaew The granddaddy of Bangkok temples and the home of a certain Emerald Buddha. (p24)

Wat Pho If you haven't seen the ginormous reclining Buddha here, you haven't seen Bangkok. (p28)

Wat Suthat Home to one of Thailand's biggest Buddhas and equally im-pressive floor-to-ceiling temple murals. (p46)

Wat Traimit Residence of the world's largest golden Buddha. (p60)

Wat Arun This pre-decessor to Bangkok is also one of the few Thai temples you're allowed to climb on. (p32)

Golden Mount & Wat Saket Hilltop temple with great views over old Bangkok. (p46)

Wat Mangkon Kamala-wat The epitome of the hectic, smoky, noisy Chinese-style temple. (p65)

Sri Mariamman Temple Bangkok's main Hindu temple practically leaps from the street. (p100)

Wat Bowonniwet Roy-ally sponsored temple with interesting murals. (p47)

Best
Gay & Lesbian

Bangkok has a notoriously pink vibe to it. From kinky male-underwear shops mushrooming at street corners to lesbian-only nightclubs, as a homosexual you could eat, shop and play here for weeks without ever leaving the comfort of gay-friendly venues.

Lesbians

Although it would be a stretch to claim that Bangkok has a lesbian scene, lesbians have become more visible in recent years, and there are a couple of lesbian-oriented bars. It's worth noting that, perhaps because Thailand is still a relatively conservative place, lesbians in Bangkok generally adhere to rather strict gender roles. Overtly 'butch' lesbians, called *tom* (from 'tomboy'), typically have short hair, bind their breasts and wear men's clothing. Femme lesbians refer to themselves as *dêe* (from 'lady'). Visiting lesbians who don't fit into one of these categories may find themselves met with confusion.

Transgender

Bangkok is famous for its open and visible transgender population – known locally as *gà·teu·i* (also spelt *kathoey*). Some are cross-dressers, while others have had sexual-reassignment surgery – Thailand is one of the leading countries for this procedure. Foreigners seem to be especially fascinated by transgender people, as they are often very convincing women, and *gà·teu·i* cabarets aimed at tourists are popular venues for observing gender-bending.

LONELY PLANET/GETTY IMAGES ©

☑ Top Tips

▶ **Bangkok Pride Festival** (www.bangkokpride.org) is the single biggest event of the gay year, and is usually held in mid-November.

▶ **Bangkok Lesbian** (www.bangkoklesbian.com) is the city's premier website for ladies who love ladies.

▶ **Utopia** (www.utopia-asia.com) publishes the *Utopia Guide to Thailand*, covering gay-friendly businesses in Bangkok.

Balcony and Telephone Pub (p94)

Best Gay & Lesbian Venues

DJ Station One of the most legendary gay dance clubs in Asia. (p95)

Zeta Bangkok's only lesbian dance club. (p113)

Telephone Pub Long-standing and perpetually popular pub right in the middle of Bangkok's pinkest zone. (p94)

G Bangkok Another booming gay dance club. (p95)

Balcony Streetside watering hole for local and visiting gays. (p94)

70's Bar Disco-themed, mostly gay dance club. (p106)

Bed Supperclub Come to this club for its popular (and pink) Confidential Sundays. (p123)

Calypso Cabaret Unapologetically campy transgender stage shows. (p86)

Nana Entertainment Plaza Hang with transgendered men at Cascades, the city's most infamous *gà·teu·i* bar. (p127)

Castro The only gay destination on the nightlife strip known as RCA. (p113)

Best
Live Music

AUSTIN BUSH/GETTY IMAGES ©

Music is an essential element of a Thai night out, and just about every pub worth its salted peanuts has a house band. For the most part this means perky Thai pop covers or international standards, but an increasing number of places have begun to deviate from the norm with quirky and/or inspired bands and performances.

Bangkok's Live Music Scene

The local matriarchs and patriarchs like dinner with an easy-listening soundtrack – typically a Filipino band and a synthesiser. An indigenous rock style, *pleng pêu·a chee·wít* (songs for life), makes appearances at a dying breed of country-and-western bars decorated with buffalo horns and pictures of Native Americans. Several dedicated bars throughout the city feature blues and rock bands, but are quite scant on live indie performances. For more subdued tastes, Bangkok also attracts grade-A jazz musicians to several hotel bars.

Best Live Music

Titanium Nightly performances by Unicorn, an all-girl band that's bound to leave you dancing. (p126)

Ad Here the 13th Closet-sized blues bar in the backpacker district. (p55)

Brick Bar Live-music den legendary among locals, for whom dancing on the tables is practically mandatory. (p53)

Raintree This earthy suburban pub – think buffalo horns as interior design – is a bastion of contemporary Thai folk music. (p91)

Saxophone Pub & Restaurant One of Bangkok's more legendary live-music venues. (p91)

Fat Gut'z Blues and, er, fish and chips – a bizarre blend that somehow works at this tiny pub. (p126)

Cotton Live jazz in Bangkok's Chinatown. (p71)

Survival Guide

Survival Guide

Before You Go

When to Go

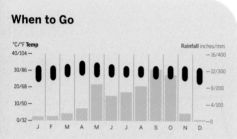

°C/°F Temp
40/104 —
30/86 —
20/68 —
10/50 —
0/32 —

J F M A M J J A S O N D

Rainfall inches/mm
— 16/400
— 12/300
— 8/200
— 4/100
—0

➡ **Winter (late Dec/early Jan)** This is both the coolest time of year in Bangkok and the peak tourist season. Consider November or February for similarly cool weather and fewer people.

➡ **Wet season (May-Oct)** During the monsoon period, Bangkok receives as much as 300mm of rain per month. The good news is that downpours are generally brief and tourist numbers are relatively low.

Book Your Stay

☑ If your idea of the typical Bangkok hotel was influenced by *The Hangover Part II*, you'll be pleased to learn that the city is home to a diverse spread of modern hostels, guesthouses and hotels. To make matters better, much of Bangkok's accommodation is excellent value, and competition is so intense that fat discounts are almost always available.

Useful Websites

➡ **Lonely Planet** (www.hotels.lonelyplanet.com) Find reviews and make bookings.

➡ **Travelfish** (www.travelfish.org) Independent reviews, lots of user feedback.

➡ **Trip Advisor** (www.tripadvisor.com) Yes, Bangkok is covered here.

➡ **Agoda** (www.agoda.com) Great advance deals.

Best Budget

➡ **Lub d** (www.lubd.com) A young-feeling, well-run hostel with two branches in central Bangkok.

➡ **NapPark Hostel** (www
.nappark.com) Hi-tech
dorm beds in a hostel
that has a distinct em-
phasis on activities.

➡ **Sam Sen Sam Place**
(www.samsensam.com)
Cutesy budget rooms in
an antique wooden home
by the river.

➡ **Suk 11** (www.suk11
.com) Rooms with an old-
school Thai vibe smack
dab in the middle of
'downtown' Bangkok.

Best Midrange

➡ **Lamphu Treehouse**
(www.lamphutreehotel.
com) Quiet, comfy,
canal-side midranger
just outside Bangkok's
backpacker zone.

➡ **Phra-Nakorn Norn-Len**
(www.phranakorn-norn
len.com) Artsy, fun hotel
compound in a refresh-
ingly untouristed 'hood.

➡ **Napa Place** (www
.napaplace.com) Modern
condo-like hotel with big
rooms and a homey vibe.

➡ **Baan Dinso** (www
.baandinso.com) An
antique villa holding basic
but attractive, boutique-
feeling rooms.

➡ **Swan Hotel** (www
.swanhotelbkk.com)
Classic '60s-era hotel
with a great pool.

➡ **72 Ekamai**
(www.72ekamai.com)
Huge, stylish rooms in an
emerging hipster 'hood.

Best Top-End

➡ **Siam Heritage** (www
.thesiamheritage.com)
Homey touches and warm
service make this this
closest you may come to
sleeping in a Thai home.

➡ **AriyasomVilla** (www
.ariyasom.com) Sumptu-
ous refurbished villa with
a classy B&B vibe.

➡ **Arun Residence** (www
.arunresidence.com)
Some of the best river
views in town; the funky,
loftlike rooms aren't too
shabby, either.

➡ **Metropolitan** (www
.comohotels.com/metro
politanbangkok) Sophisti-
cated urban cool in the
centre of the city.

Arriving in Bangkok

Air

**Suvarnabhumi Interna-
tional Airport**

Just about everybody
flying to Bangkok comes

through **Suvarnabhumi
International Airport**
(☎0 2132 1888; www
.bangkokairportonline.com),
located 25km east of the
city centre. Pronounced
sù·wan·ná·poom, the airport is accessible by taxi
and public transport –
including the **Airport Rail
Link** (www.bangkokairport
train.com) – and estimated
transit time to most parts
of Bangkok is approxi-
mately 30 to 45 minutes.
A taxi to central Bangkok
will run about 300B.
The unofficial website
has real-time details
of airport arrivals and
departures. Left-luggage
facilities are available on
level 2, beside the helpful
Tourism Authority of
Thailand office.

Don Muang Airport

Bangkok's former
international airport, **Don
Muang** (DMK; ☎0 2535
1111; www.donmuangair
portonline.com), has been
downgraded to the city's
de facto low-cost airport.
It's located about 20km
north of the city centre;
slow buses make the
trip into town, but taxi is
the most efficient way to
get to/from the airport,
and to central Bangkok
should cost around
200B.

Train

Hualamphong Train Station (📞 0 2220 4334, nationwide call centre 1690; www.railway.co.th; off Th Phra Ram IV) is the city's main train terminal, and is linked to the the MRT (metro) stop at Hua Lamphong.

Bus

Main bus terminals include **Northern & Northeastern Bus Terminal** (Mor Chit; 📞 northeastern routes 0 2936 2852, ext 611/448, northern routes 0 2936 2841, ext 311/442; Th Kamphaeng Phet; Ⓜ Kamphaeng Phet exit 1 & taxi, Ⓢ Mo Chit exit 3 & taxi), **Eastern Bus Terminal** (Ekamai; 📞 0 2391 2504; Soi 40, Th Sukhumvit; Ⓢ Ekkamai exit 2) and **Southern Bus Terminal** (Sai Tai Mai; 📞 0 2435 1199; Th Bromaratchachonanee), all at different ends of the city, and all conveniently linked to the various parts of town by taxi.

Travel Passes

Both the BTS and MRT offer one-day unlimited-ride passes for 120B.

Getting Around

BTS & MRT

☑ **Best for...** Getting between points in central Bangkok and getting around during peak hours.

The elevated **BTS** (📞 0 2617 7300, tourist information 0 2617 7340; www.bts.co.th), also known as the Skytrain, whisks you through 'new' Bangkok (Silom, Sukhumvit and Siam Sq). The interchange is at Siam station, and trains run frequently 6am to midnight. Fares range from 15B to 55B. Most ticket machines only accept coins; change is available at the info booths.

Bangkok's **MRT** (www .bangkokmetro.co.th), or metro, helps people staying in the Sukhumvit or Silom area reach Chinatown or the train station at Hualamphong. Fares cost 16B to 40B. The trains run frequently from 6am to midnight.

Taxi

☑ **Best for...** Getting from one part of town to another at non-peak hours.

Many first-time visitors are hesitant to use them, but in general taxis are

new and comfortable and the drivers are courteous and helpful, making them an excellent way to get around.

All taxis are required to use their meters, which start at 35B, and fares to most places within central Bangkok cost 60B to 90B. Freeway tolls – 25B to 45B depending on where you start – must be paid by the passenger.

Taxi Radio (📞 1681; www.taxiradio.co.th) and other 24-hour 'phone-a-cab' services are available for 20B above the metered fare.

Boat

☑ **Best for...** Slowly but surely jumping between the tourist sights in Banglamphu, Ko Ratanakosin and parts of Silom.

The **Chao Phraya Express Boat** (📞 0 2623 6001; chaophrayaexpressboat.com) runs from 6am to 8pm on weekdays and from 6am to 7pm on weekends. You can buy tickets (10B to 32B) at the pier or on board; hold on to your ticket as proof of purchase. Boats with yellow or red-and-orange flags are express boats. These run only during peak times and don't make every stop

A yellow-flagged tourist boat runs from Tha Sathon (Central Pier) to Tha Phra Athit (Banglamphu) with stops at 10 major sight-seeing piers and barely comprehensible English-language commentary.

There are also dozens of cross-river ferries, which charge 3B and run every few minutes until late at night.

Klorng (canal, also spelled *khlong*) taxi boats run along Khlong Saen Saeb (Banglamphu to Ramkhamhaeng) and are an easy way to get between Banglamphu and Jim Thompson's House, the Siam Sq shopping centres and other points further east along Th Sukhumvit – after a mandatory change of boat at Tha Pratunam. These boats are mostly used by daily commuters and pull into the piers for just a few seconds – jump straight on or you'll be left behind. Fares range from 9B to 21B and boats run from 6.15am to 7.30pm.

Motorcycle Taxi

☑ **Best for...** Getting to the end of a long street or getting somewhere in a hurry during peak hours.

Motorcycle taxis (known as *motorsai*) serve two purposes in Bangkok. Most commonly and popularly they form an integral part of the public-transport network, running from the corner of a main thoroughfare, such as Th Sukhumvit, to the far ends of soi that run off that thoroughfare. Riders wear coloured, numbered vests and gather at either end of their soi, usually charging 10B to 20B for the trip (without a helmet unless you ask). Their other purpose is as a means of beating the traffic. You tell your rider where you want to go, negotiate a price (from 20B for a short trip up to about 150B for going across town), strap on the helmet (they will insist for longer trips) and say a prayer to whichever god you're into.

Túk-Túk

☑ **Best for...** Short hops within a neighbourhood.

These putt-putting three-wheeled vehicles are irresistible tourist-traps – they'll zip you to an over-priced tailor or jeweller regardless of your stated destination. Refuse to enter any unrequested shop, and skip the 10B sightseeing offers.

Bus

☑ **Best for...** Reaching Banglamphu, Dusit and other areas not serviced by the BTS or MRT.

Bangkok's public buses are run by the **Bangkok Mass Transit Authority** (☎ 0 2246 0973; www.bmta .co.th). As the routes are not always clear, and with Bangkok taxis being such a good deal, you'd really have to be pinching pennies to rely on buses as a way to get around Bangkok. However, if you're determined, air-con bus fares range from 11B to 23B, and fares for fan-cooled buses start at 7B or 8B. Most of the bus lines run between 5am and 10pm or 11pm.

Essential Information

Business Hours

Opening hours for businesses in this book are listed only if they differ from the following.

➡ **Banks** From 8.30am to 3.30pm Monday to Friday; banks in shopping centres and tourist areas often open longer hours (generally until 8pm), including weekends.

➡ Bars & Clubs Open until midnight or 1am, although those in designated entertainment zones can stay open until 2am or 3am.

➡ Restaurants Local places often serve food from morning to night (10am to 8pm or 9pm), while more formal restaurants serve only during lunch (from around 11am to 2pm) and dinner (6pm to 10pm).

➡ Shops Large shops usually open from 10am to 7pm; shopping centres open until 10pm.

Electricity

120V/60Hz

120V/60Hz

Emergencies

➡ Ambulance (☎ via police 191) In a medical emergency, it's probably best to call a hospital direct, and it will dispatch an ambulance.

➡ Tourist Police (☎24hr hotline 1155) The best way to deal with most problems requiring police (usually a rip-off or theft) is to contact the tourist police, who can generally communicate in English, are used to dealing with foreigners and can be very helpful in cases of arrest.

Money

➡ Currency The basic unit of Thai currency is the baht. There are 100 satang in one baht. Coins come in denominations of 25 satang, 50 satang, 1B, 2B, 5B and 10B. Paper currency comes in denominations of 20B (green), 50B (blue), 100B (red), 500B (purple) and 1000B (beige).

➡ ATMs You won't need a map to find an ATM in Bangkok – they're literally everywhere. ATMs accept major international credit cards and many will also cough up cash (Thai baht only) if your card is affiliated with the international Cirrus or Plus networks (typically for a fee of 150B). You can withdraw up to 20,000B per day from most ATMs.

➡ Credit cards Credit cards as well as debit cards can be used for purchases at many shops and pretty much any hotel or restaurant, though you'll have to pay cash for your pàt tai. The most commonly accepted cards are Visa and MasterCard, followed by Amex and JCB.

➡ Money changers Banks or legal money-changers offer the optimum foreign-exchange rates. When buying baht, US dollars and euros are the most readily accepted currencies, and travellers cheques receive better rates than cash. British pounds, Australian dollars, Singapore dollars and Hong Kong dollars are also widely accepted.

➡ **Tipping** Tipping is not a traditional part of Thai life and, except in big hotels and posh restaurants, tips are appreciated but not expected.

Public Holidays

Government offices and banks close their doors on the following national public holidays. For the precise dates of lunar holidays, see the Tourism Authority of Thailand (TAT) website, www.tourismthailand.org/See-and-Do/Events-and-Festivals.

➡ **New Year's Day** 1 January

➡ **Makha Bucha Day** January/March (lunar)

➡ **Chakri Day** Commemorates the founding of the royal Chakri dynasty; 6 April

➡ **Songkran** Thai New Year; 13-15 April

➡ **Labor Day** 1 May

➡ **Coronation Day** Commemorating the 1950 coronation of the current king and queen; 5 May

➡ **Visakha Bucha Day** May/June (lunar)

➡ **Khao Phansa** Beginning of the Buddhist rains retreat, when monks refrain from travelling away from their monasteries; July/August (lunar)

➡ **Queen's Birthday** 12 August

➡ **King Chulalongkorn Day** 23 October

➡ **Ok Phansa** End of Buddhist rains retreat; October/November (lunar)

➡ **King's Birthday** 5 December

➡ **Constitution Day** 10 December

➡ **New Year's Eve** 31 December

Safe Travel

Bangkok is generally a safe city and violence against tourists is rare. That said, there are enough well-rehearsed scams that there's an entire website (www.bangkokscams.com) dedicated to them. Don't be spooked by the stories; commit the following to memory and you'll likely enjoy a scam-free visit:

➡ **Gem scam** We're begging you, if you aren't a gem trader or expert, then please don't buy unset stones in Thailand – period. Otherwise, you'll find yourself getting sucked into a complicated scam in which you'll pay an exorbitant price for costume jewellery.

➡ **Closed today** Ignore any 'friendly' local who tells you that an attraction is closed for a Buddhist holiday or for cleaning. These are set-ups for trips to a bogus gem sale.

➡ **Túk-túk rides for 10B** Say goodbye to your day's itinerary if you climb aboard this ubiquitous scam. These alleged 'tours' bypass all the sights and instead cruise to all the fly-by-night gem and tailor shops that pay commissions.

➡ **Flat-fare taxi ride** Flatly refuse any taxi driver who quotes a flat fare (usually between 100B and 150B for in-town destinations), which will usually be three times more expensive than the reasonable meter rate. Walking beyond the tourist area will usually help you find an honest driver.

➡ **Friendly strangers** Be wary of smartly dressed,

well-spoken men who approach you asking where you're from and where you're going. This is usually followed with: 'Ah, my son/daughter is studying at university in (your home city)' – they seem to have an encyclopaedic knowledge of the world's major universities. As the tourist authorities here have pointed out, this sort of behaviour is out of character for Thais and should be treated with suspicion.

Telephone

Mobile Phones

If you have a GSM phone you'll probably be able to use it on roaming in Thailand. If you have endless cash, or you only want to send text messages, you might be happy to do that. Otherwise, think about buying a local SIM card.

If your phone is locked, get it unlocked or shop for a new or cheap used phone (starting at less than 1000B).

Buying a prepaid SIM is as easy as finding a 7-Eleven. The market is super-competitive and deals vary so check websites first, but expect to get a SIM for as little as 49B. More expensive SIMs

might come with preloaded talk time; if not, recharge cards are sold at the same stores and range from 100B to 500B.

Making International & Domestic Calls

Inside Thailand you must dial the area code no matter where you are. In effect, that means all numbers are nine digits; in Bangkok they begin with 02, and are followed by a seven-digit number. The only time you drop the initial 0 is when you're calling from outside Thailand.

To direct-dial an international number from a private phone, you can dial 001 then the country code.But you wouldn't do that, because 001 is the most expensive way to call internationally, and numerous other prefixes give you cheaper rates. These include 006, 007, 008 and 009, depending on which phone you're calling from. If you buy a local mobile-phone SIM card, the network provider will tell you which prefix to use; read the fine print.

Useful Numbers

➡ **Thailand country code** 66

➡ **Bangkok city code** 02

➡ **Mobile numbers** 08, 09

➡ **Operator-assisted international calls** 100

➡ **Free local directory assistance call** 1133

Toilets

If you don't want to pee against a tree like the túk-túk drivers, you can stop in at any shopping centre, hotel or fast-food restaurant for facilities. Shopping centres typically charge 2B to 3B for a visit.

In older buildings and wát you'll still find squat toilets, but in modern Bangkok expect to be greeted by a throne.

Toilet paper is rarely provided, so carry an emergency stash. Even in places where sit-down toilets are installed, the septic system may not be designed to take toilet paper. In such cases there will be a waste basket where you're supposed to place used toilet paper and feminine hygiene products. Many toilets also come with a small spray hose – Thailand's version of the bidet.

Tourist Information

Bangkok has two organisations that handle tourism matters: the Tourism Authority of Thailand

(TAT) for country-wide information, and Bangkok Information Center for city-specific information.

⮕ **Bangkok Information Center** (☏ 0 2225 7612-4; www.bangkoktourist.com; 17/1 Th Phra Athit; ⏰ 8am-7pm Mon-Fri, 9am-5pm Sat & Sun; ⛴ Tha Phra Athit) City-specific tourism office that provides maps, brochures and directions. Kiosks and booths are found around town; look for the green-on-white symbol of a mahout on an elephant.

⮕ **Tourism Authority of Thailand** (TAT; ☏ 1672; www.tourismthailand.org) **head office** (☏ 0 2250 5500; 1600 Th Phetch-aburi Tat Mai, Sukhumvit; ⏰ 8.30am-4.30pm; Ⓜ Phet-chaburi exit 2); **Banglam-phu** (☏ 0 2283 1500; cnr Th Ratchadamnoen Nok & Th Chakrapatdipong; ⏰ 8.30am-4.30pm; ⛴ Tha Phan Fah); **Suvarnabhumi Interna-tional Airport** (☏ 0 2134 0040; 2nd fl, btwn gates 2 & 5, Suvarnabhumi International Airport; ⏰ 24hr).

Travellers with Disabilities

With its high kerbs, uneven pavements and non-stop traffic Bangkok presents one large, ongoing

Dos & Don'ts

⮕ Don't say anything critical about the Thai royal family.

⮕ Do dress respectfully at royal buildings and temples.

⮕ Don't wear your shoes indoors.

⮕ Do try to avoid conflict or raising your voice with locals.

⮕ Don't touch another person's head.

obstacle course for the mobility-impaired. Many of the city's streets must be crossed via pedestrian bridges flanked with steep stairways, while buses and boats don't stop long enough to accommodate even the mildly disabled. Apart from some BTS and MRT stations, ramps or other access points for wheelchairs are rare.

A few top-end hotels make consistent design efforts to provide disabled access. Other deluxe hotels with high employee-to-guest ratios are usually good about providing staff help where building design fails. For the rest, you're pretty much left to your own resources.

The following compa-nies and websites might be useful: **Asia Pacific Development Centre on Disability** (www.apcd

foundation.org), **Society for Accessible Travel & Hospitality** (SATH; www .sath.org), and **Wheelchair Tours to Thailand** (www .wheelchairtours.com).

Visas

Thailand's **Ministry of Foreign Affairs** (www .mfa.go.th) oversees immigration and visa issues. In the past five years there have been new rules nearly every year regarding visas and extensions; the best on-line monitor is **Thaivisa** (www.thaivisa.com).

Citizens of 41 coun-tries (including most European countries, Australia, New Zealand and the USA) can enter Thailand at no charge. These citizens are issued a 30-day visa if they arrive by air or 15 days if they arrive by land.

Language

In Thai the meaning of a single syllable may be altered by means of different tones. Standard Thai has five tones: low (eg *bàht*), mid (eg *dee*), falling (eg *mâi*), high (eg *máh*) and rising (eg *săhm*). The range of all five tones is relative to each speaker's vocal range, so there is no fixed 'pitch' intrinsic to the language.

Read our pronunciation guides as if they were English and you'll be understood. The hyphens indicate syllable breaks; some syllables are further divided with a dot to help you pronounce compound vowels (eg *mêu·a·rai*). Note that **b** is a hard 'p' sound, almost like a 'b' (eg in 'hip-bag'); **d** is a hard 't' sound, like a sharp 'd' (eg in 'mid-tone'); **ng** is pronounced as in 'singing', but in Thai it can also occur at the start of a word; and **r** is pronounced as in 'run' but flapped, and in everyday speech it's often pronounced like 'l'.

To enhance your trip with a phrasebook, visit **lonelyplanet.com**. Lonely Planet iPhone phrasebooks are available through the Apple App store.

Basics

Hello.	สวัสดี	sà-wàt-dee
Goodbye.	ลาก่อน	lah gòrn
Yes./No.	ใช่/ไม่	châi/mâi
Please.	ขอ	kŏr
Thank you.	ขอบคุณ	kòrp kun
You're welcome.	ยินดี	yin dee
Excuse me.	ขออภัย	kŏr à-pai
Sorry.	ขอโทษ	kŏr tôht

How are you?

สบายดีไหม   sà-bai dee măi

Fine. And you?

สบายดีครับ/ค่า/   sà-bai dee kráp/
แล้วคุณล่ะ   kâ láa·ou kun lâ (m/f)

Do you speak English?

คุณพูดภาษา   kun pôot pah-săh
อังกฤษได้ไหม   ang-grìt dâi măi

I don't understand.

ผม/ดิฉันไม่   pŏm/dì-chăn mâi
เข้าใจ   kôw jai (m/f)

Eating & Drinking

I'd like (the menu), please.

ขอ (รายการ   kŏr (rai gahn
อาหาร) หน่อย   ah-hăhn) nòy

I don't eat ...

ผม/ดิฉัน   pŏm/dì-chăn
ไม่กิน ...   mâi gin ... (m/f)

eggs	ไข่	kài
fish	ปลา	blah
red meat	เนื้อแดง	néu·a daang
nuts	ถั่ว	tòo·a

That was delicious!

อร่อยมาก   à-ròy mâhk

Cheers!

ไชโย   chai-yoh

Please bring the bill.

ขอบิลหน่อย   kŏr bin nòy

cafe	ร้านกาแฟ	ráhn gah-faa
market	ตลาด	đà-làht
restaurant	ร้านอาหาร	ráhn ah-hǎhn
vegetarian	คนกินเจ	kon gin jair

Meat & Fish

beef	เนื้อ	néu·a
chicken	ไก่	gài
crab	ปู	boo
duck	เป็ด	bèt
fish	ปลา	blah
meat	เนื้อ	néu·a
pork	หมู	mǒo
seafood	อาหารทะเล	ah-hǎhn tá-lair
squid	ปลาหมึก	blah mèuk

Fruit & Vegetables

banana	กล้วย	glôo·ay
beans	ถั่ว	tòo·a
coconut	มะพร้าว	má-prów
eggplant	มะเขือ	má-kěu·a
fruit	ผลไม้	pǒn-lá-mái
guava	ฝรั่ง	fa-ràng
lime	มะนาว	má-now
mango	มะม่วง	má-môo·ang
mangosteen	มังคุด	mang-kút
mushrooms	เห็ด	hèt
nuts	ถั่ว	tòo·a
papaya	มะละกอ	má-lá-gor
potatoes	มันฝรั่ง	man fa-ràng
rambutan	เงาะ	ngó
tamarind	มะขาม	má-kǎhm
tomatoes	มะเขือเทศ	má-kěu·a têt
vegetables	ผัก	pàk
watermelon	แตงโม	đaang moh

Drinks

beer	เบียร์	bee·a
coffee	กาแฟ	gah-faa
milk	นมจืด	nom jèut
orange juice	น้ำส้ม	nám sôm
soy milk	น้ำเต้าหู้	nám đôw hôo
sugar-cane juice	น้ำอ้อย	nám ôy
tea	ชา	chah
water	น้ำดื่ม	nám dèum

Other

chilli	พริก	prík
egg	ไข่	kài
fish sauce	น้ำปลา	nám blah
noodles	เส้น	sên
pepper	พริกไทย	prík tai
rice	ข้าว	kôw
salad	ผักสด	pàk sòt
salt	เกลือ	gleu·a
soup	น้ำซุป	nám súp
soy sauce	น้ำซีอิ้ว	nám see-éw
sugar	น้ำตาล	nám đahn
tofu	เต้าหู้	đôw hôo

Shopping

I'd like to buy ...
อยากจะซื้อ ...	yàhk jà séu ...

How much is it?
เท่าไร	tôw-rai

That's too expensive.
แพงไป	paang bai

Can you lower the price?
ลดราคาได้ไหม	lót rah-kah dâi măi

There's a mistake in the bill.
บิลใบนี้ผิด	bin bai née pìt ná
นะครับ/ค่ะ	kráp/kâ (m/f)

Emergencies

Help!	ช่วยด้วย	chôo·ay dôo·ay

Go away!	ไปให้พ้น	bai hâi pón

Call a doctor!
เรียกหมอหน่อย	rêe·ak mŏr nòy

Call the police!
เรียกตำรวจหน่อย	rêe·ak đam·ròo·at nòy

I'm ill.
ผม/ดิฉัน	pŏm/dì·chăn
ป่วย	bòo·ay (m/f)

I'm lost.
ผม/ดิฉัน	pŏm/dì·chăn
หลงทาง	lŏng tahng (m/f)

Where are the toilets?
ห้องน้ำอยู่ที่ไหน	hôrng nám yòo têe năi

Time, Days & Numbers

What time is it?
กี่โมงแล้ว	gèe mohng láa·ou

morning	เช้า	chów
afternoon	บ่าย	bài
evening	เย็น	yen
yesterday	เมื่อวาน	mêu·a wahn
today	วันนี้	wan née
tomorrow	พรุ่งนี้	prûng née
Monday	วันจันทร์	wan jan
Tuesday	วันอังคาร	wan ang-kahn
Wednesday	วันพุธ	wan pút
Thursday	วันพฤหัสฯ	wan pá-réu-hàt
Friday	วันศุกร	wan sùk
Saturday	วันเสาร์	wan sŏw
Sunday	วันอาทิตย์	wan ah-tít
1	หนึ่ง	nèung
2	สอง	sŏrng
3	สาม	săhm
4	สี่	sèe
5	ห้า	hâh
6	หก	hòk
7	เจ็ด	jèt
8	แปด	bàat
9	เก้า	gôw
10	สิบ	sìp
20	ยี่สิบ	yêe-sìp
21	ยี่สิบเอ็ด	yêe-sìp-èt

30	สามสิบ	sǎhm-sìp
40	สี่สิบ	sèe-sìp
50	ห้าสิบ	hâh-sìp
60	หกสิบ	hòk-sìp
70	เจ็ดสิบ	jèt-sìp
80	แปดสิบ	bàat-sìp
90	เก้าสิบ	gôw-sìp
100	หนึ่งร้อย	nèung róy
1000	หนึ่งพัน	nèung pan
1,000,000	หนึ่งล้าน	nèung láhn

Transport & Directions

Where is ...?

... อยู่ที่ไหน ... yòo têe nǎi

What's the address?

ที่อยู่คืออะไร têe yòo keu à-rai

Can you show me (on the map)?

ให้ดู (ในแผนที่) hâi doo (nai pǎen têe)

ได้ไหม dâi mǎi

Turn left/right.

เลี้ยวซ้าย/ขวา lée·o sái/kwǎh

bicycle rickshaw	สามล้อ	sǎhm lór
boat	เรือ	reu·a
bus	รถเมล์	rót mair
car	รถเก๋ง	rót gěng
motorcycle	มอร์เตอร์ไซค์	mor-đeu-sai
taxi	รับจ้าง	ráp jâhng
plane	เครื่องบิน	krêu·ang bin
train	รถไฟ	rót fai
túk-túk	ตุ๊ก ๆ	đúk đúk

When's the first bus?

รถเมล์คันแรก rót mair kan râak

มาเมื่อไร mah mêu·a rai

A (one-way/return) ticket, please.

ขอตั๋ว (เที่ยว kǒr đǒo·a (têe·o

ดียว/ไปกลับ). dee·o/bai glàp)

What time does it get to ...?

ถึง ... กี่โมง těung ... gèe mohng

Does it stop at ...?

รถจอดที่ ... ไหม rót jòrt têe ... mǎi

I'd like to get off at ...

ขอลงที่ ... kǒr long têe ...

Behind the Scenes

Send Us Your Feedback

We love to hear from travellers – your comments help make our books better. We read every word, and we guarantee that your feedback goes straight to the authors. Visit **lonelyplanet.com/contact** to submit your updates and suggestions.

Note: We may edit, reproduce and incorporate your comments in Lonely Planet products such as guidebooks, websites and digital products, so let us know if you don't want your comments reproduced or your name acknowledged. For a copy of our privacy policy visit lonelyplanet.com/privacy.

Our Readers

Many thanks to the travellers who used the last edition and wrote to us with helpful hints, useful advice and interesting anecdotes:
Astrid de Koning, Sarah Shafaghi

Austin's Thanks

I'd like to thank the folks at Lonely Planet, in particular the patient and helpful Ilaria Walker; this book's original author, China Williams; the kind people on the ground here in Bangkok; and *khao khluk kapi* for being so delicious.

Acknowledgments

Cover photograph: Wat Arun, Bangkok, Gavin Hellier/AWL.

This Book

This 4th edition of Lonely Planet's *Pocket Bangkok* guidebook was researched and written by Austin Bush, who also wrote the previous two editions. This guidebook was commissioned in Lonely Planet's Melbourne office, and produced by the following:

Commissioning Editor Ilaria Walker **Coordinating Editors** Kate James, Simon Williamson **Coordinating Cartographer** Xavier Di Toro **Coordinating Layout Designer** Kerrianne Southway **Managing Editors** Barbara Delissen, Martine Power **Senior Editor** Andi Jones **Managing Cartographers** Anita Banh, Diana Von Holdt

Managing Layout Designer Chris Girdler **Cover Research** Naomi Parker **Internal Image Research** Kylie McLaughlin **Language Content** Branislava Vladisavljevic **Thanks to** Bruce Evans, Ryan Evans, Larissa Frost, Genesys India, Jouve India, Trent Paton, Raphael Richards, Gerard Walker

Index

See also separate subindexes for:

✪ **Eating p177**

🍷 **Drinking p178**

✪ **Entertainment p178**

🏠 **Shopping p179**

Sights p000
Map Pages p000

Sights p000
Map Pages p000

Our Writer

Austin Bush

Austin Bush came to Thailand in 1999 as part of a language
scholarship hosted by Chiang Mai University. The lure of
city life, employment and spicy food eventually led Austin to
Bangkok and have managed to keep him there since. He's a
native of Oregon and a writer and photographer who often
focuses on food; samples of his work can be seen at www.
austinbushphotography.com.

Published by Lonely Planet Publications Pty Ltd
ABN 36 005 607 983
4th edition – June 2013
ISBN 978 1 74220 304 1
© Lonely Planet 2013   Photographs © as indicated 2013
10 9 8 7 6 5 4 3 2 1
Printed in China